Improve Your Opening

Are your partners in the habit of describing your leads as inspired, brilliant or devastating? Then you will have no use for this book. But if the adjectives that spring to your partners' lips are less flattering, a study of these problems will be worth your while. Improved leading will make a startling difference to your defence and to your whole bridge game.

In selecting the opening lead a player makes a decision that often influences the entire course of the defence for good or ill. With the aid of fifty examples, the authors show how the expert mind works in this situation, explaining how to interpret the bidding, how to visualise the opponents' hands and how to weigh up the conflicting factors that are involved in every choice of lead.

Hugh Kelsey, grand master, international player and Gold Cup winner is well known as the author of many best-selling books on bridge. Co-author John Matheson is one of the brightest stars in the Scottish bridge firmament. Dr Matheson is also a Gold Cup winner and has managed to spare the time from his busy medical practice near Glasgow to represent Scotland twelve times in international matches.

Also by
HUGH KELSEY

Instant Guide To Bridge
Slam Bidding
Winning Card Play
Adventures in Card Play
(with Géza Ottlik)

Improve Your
Opening Leads

HUGH KELSEY
and
JOHN MATHESON

LONDON
VICTOR GOLLANCZ LTD
in association with Peter Crawley
1979

© *Hugh Kelsey and John Matheson 1979*
ISBN 0 575 02657 X

Printed in Great Britain by
Lowe and Brydone Printers Ltd., Thetford, Norfolk

Contents

Introduction

Of the thousands of bridge books that have been published over the years, few have been devoted to the opening lead. This is understandable, for it is a difficult subject to present except in elementary form. Yet the importance of the first blow by the defenders can hardly be overstated. It is possible that more points are chucked on the opening lead than in any other phase of the game.

In a sense the opening lead provides a complete test of a bridge player's ability. It takes a good bidder to interpret correctly the inferences from the opponents' bidding, it takes imagination and card sense to project from the bidding what is likely to happen in the play of the hand, and it takes a knowledge of practical psychology to assess an opponent's reliability and to anticipate his reaction to any particular lead.

A factor that has to be taken into account is the form of scoring. At match-point pairs, where an overtrick can make the difference between a top and a bottom, the experienced defender leans towards safety when a close decision has to be made, selecting the lead that is less likely to concede a cheap trick. At rubber bridge or in a team game he tends to lead more aggressively.

In this book we present a study of the opening lead through the medium of fifty examples. The reader is shown the West hand and the bidding, and has the chance to work out his own answer before going on to read the analysis and turning the page to see the complete hand. These illustrative hands are given not to prove that our own answers are correct (indeed, in some cases the recommended lead bites the dust) but to serve as a point of reference for the reader.

We have awarded marks out of ten for each lead that we judge to have some merit. This is a convenient way of stating not only our order of preference but also whether we consider one lead to be markedly superior to another. Inevitably this method of assessment is subjective and somewhat arbitrary, but we feel that readers will wish to be given a definitive answer in each case.

The fifty examples have been grouped in seven sections, but many of the hands might have been classified under a different heading and readers should not expect to find a clue to the solution of a problem in the title of the chapter.

With ten marks available on each problem, the maximum possible is five hundred, and readers may care to keep a running score for their own amusement. An experienced player should manage to finish above the half-way mark, and a rough grading could be made as follows:

251–300	— County Leader
301–350	— National Leader
351–400	— Master Leader
401 or more	— Champion Leader

Whether you score well or not, we hope that you enjoy the book and derive some profit from it.

1
Active or Passive?

On many hands the first decision a defender has to make is whether to adopt an active or a passive policy. When it appears that the opponents have stretched to the limit and have nothing in reserve, it may pay to make a neutral lead, giving nothing away and letting the contract run its course. Conversely, when the indications are that the declarer will have little difficulty in developing the tricks he needs if left to his own devices, it may be necessary to take risks, leading away from unsupported honours in an attempt to set up fast tricks for the defence.

The biggest asset a defender can possess is a flexible mind capable of judging each situation on its merits.

PROBLEM 1

E–W game.   Team of four.
Dealer South.

West holds   *The bidding*

♠ 10 9 4 3   W   N   E   S
♡ A Q 10 2   1S
◇ Q 10 7   —   2S   —   4S
♣ 8 6   all pass

Analysis

Here the passive leads are a trump or a club, the active leads a diamond or a heart.

The opponents will have eight or nine trumps on this auction and the lead of a low trump is not likely to cost a trick even if partner has a singleton honour. Dummy may well have some ruffing values, for the response on a flat moderate hand would have been one no trump. A trump lead could be beneficial in these circumstances, and you have potential entries to enable you to persist with trump leads.

A club lead would also be passive and it might enable you to obtain a ruff, although partner will not be too rich in entries.

With length in trumps, of course, it is normal to play an active, forcing defence in an attempt to shorten declarer's trumps, but here you have no obvious suit in which to force. A diamond lead could be right if declarer has a black two-suiter, but you would need to find partner with several useful diamonds. If you are thinking of a force the ace of hearts is better in a sense, requiring only one specific card in the suit from partner. However, the heart lead is more likely to give away a trick.

[13]

Strong two-suiters are less common than strong all-round hands, and the indications seem to favour the choice of as passive a lead as possible.

Marks	Small trump	10
	Club eight	8
	Heart ace	2
	Diamond seven	2

Full hand

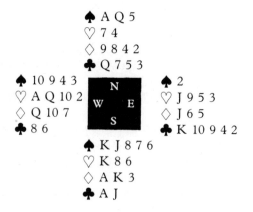

```
              ♠ A Q 5
              ♡ 7 4
              ♢ 9 8 4 2
              ♣ Q 7 5 3
♠ 10 9 4 3                    ♠ 2
♡ A Q 10 2        N           ♡ J 9 5 3
♢ Q 10 7      W     E         ♢ J 6 5
♣ 8 6            S            ♣ K 10 9 4 2
              ♠ K J 8 7 6
              ♡ K 8 6
              ♢ A K 3
              ♣ A J
```

This hand was originally set as a play problem—on a club lead declarer must play hearts from his own hand to make sure of his ruff in dummy. Three no trumps by South is, of course, a superior contract.

PROBLEM 2

Love all.   Rubber bridge with a good partner
Dealer East.   against moderate opponents.

West holds   *The bidding*

	W	N	E	S
♠ A 10 8 5 2			—	1NT(15–17)
♡ 9 5 4	—	3C*	—	3D*
◇ 7 6 3	—	3H*	—	3NT
♣ 10 7	—	6NT	all pass	
			* *Natural*	

Analysis

A lead of either red suit may be required from an active point of view. Partner could have the heart king behind dummy's ace, for instance, in which case it would take a heart lead to establish the king before the ace of spades is driven out. A similar argument can be advanced for a diamond lead, although declarer is more likely to hold the diamond ace than the heart ace.

The case for a club is much weaker, for it must be unlikely that declarer can run twelve tricks without tackling the clubs himself. And a club lead could be disastrous if partner has the queen.

What about a spade? The lead of a low spade would be routine against three no trumps; could it be right against six no trumps? There is an obvious risk of giving declarer his twelfth trick when partner has the queen and jack of spades, and of saving him a guess when partner has only the queen. Another possibility is to lead the ace of spades—you may have the ace and king to cash, but then the lead of a low spade will do as well.

[15]

Strangely enough, in spite of the risks, a small spade is probably the most passive lead. It will not normally cost a trick when partner has the nine or the jack, whereas the lead of the ace would.

Marks

Small spade	10
Ace of spades	6
Heart	6
Diamond	3
Club	1

Full hand

```
                   ♠ 6 4
                   ♡ A K Q 3
                   ◇ J 4
                   ♣ A Q J 9 3
   ♠ A 10 8 5 2                    ♠ K 3
   ♡ 9 5 4          N              ♡ 10 7 6
   ◇ 7 6 3      W       E          ◇ 10 9 8 5
   ♣ 10 7           S              ♣ 8 6 5 4
                   ♠ Q J 9 7
                   ♡ J 8 2
                   ◇ A K Q 2
                   ♣ K 2
```

PROBLEM 3

| N–S game. | Team of four. |
| Dealer South. | |

| *West holds* | *The bidding* |

<table>
<tr><td>♠ 8 2</td><td>W</td><td>N</td><td>E</td><td>S</td></tr>
<tr><td>♡ 8 6 4</td><td></td><td></td><td></td><td>—</td></tr>
<tr><td>◇ A 9 4</td><td>—</td><td>1C</td><td>—</td><td>1S</td></tr>
<tr><td>♣ K 10 9 5 2</td><td>—</td><td>2C</td><td>—</td><td>2H</td></tr>
<tr><td></td><td>—</td><td>4H</td><td colspan="2">all pass</td></tr>
</table>

Analysis

North cannot have great high-card strength in view of his minimum rebid in clubs, yet he leapt to four hearts. He is likely to have six clubs and four hearts. East is marked with some values and he can hardly be void in clubs—that would give him eleven cards in spades and diamonds and at this vulnerability he would surely have found a bid over one club. If anyone is void in clubs it will be declarer, and a club lead is likely to help him.

There is a case for an active diamond lead, for declarer may be able to discard losing diamonds from dummy on his spades. However, the lead of the ace of diamonds could easily give away a trick or a vital tempo.

There can be no point in leading a spade—any trick for the defence in this suit surely cannot disappear.

The normal lead when the opponents have found a fit in a third suit is a trump, and the indications are very strong here. You have nuisance values in clubs and East will have length in spades. Furthermore, you can see that a cross-ruff will go well for declarer since neither defender will be able to over-ruff at any point. The passive trump lead is marked.

[17]

Marks A trump   10
         Ace of diamonds   4
         Five of clubs   1

Full hand

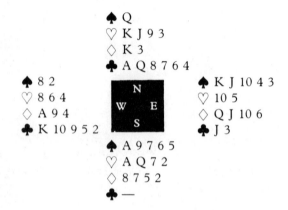

```
                    ♠ Q
                    ♡ K J 9 3
                    ◇ K 3
                    ♣ A Q 8 7 6 4
  ♠ 8 2              N            ♠ K J 10 4 3
  ♡ 8 6 4       W       E        ♡ 10 5
  ◇ A 9 4           S            ◇ Q J 10 6
  ♣ K 10 9 5 2                   ♣ J 3
                    ♠ A 9 7 6 5
                    ♡ A Q 7 2
                    ◇ 8 7 5 2
                    ♣ —
```

Active or Passive?

PROBLEM 4

E–W game.	Rubber bridge against
Dealer North.	competent but not expert
	opponents.

West holds

♠ 10 9 4
♡ 10 9 6 5
♢ A J 10 2
♣ A K

The bidding

W	N	E	S
	1C	—	1S
—	3S	—	4S
all pass			

Analysis

You could try for four tricks in a hurry by starting with the top clubs. Then, even if dummy has a singleton diamond, you may be able to put partner in with the king to give you a club ruff. If you normally lead the ace from A K x you should reverse the order here to alert partner to the fact that you have a doubleton. However, cashing a top club will often give up an important tempo, enabling declarer to draw trumps and knock out your second club stopper while he still has control in the other suits.

A trump lead may or may not cost a trick. In certain circumstances the lead of the nine of spades could give you an increased chance of a trump trick—when declarer has something like A J 8 x opposite Q x x x. But the clubs are so well placed for declarer that a trump lead looks far too passive.

A heart lead could produce an eventual force on dummy, and the rank of your trumps may assume significance if declarer has to ruff hearts in dummy.

The lead of the ace of diamonds might have a similar effect

if dummy's shortage is in diamonds, but this is a dangerous lead—much more likely to give away tricks than a heart.

Marks

A heart	10
Club ace or king	7
Diamond ace	3
Nine of spades	2

Full hand

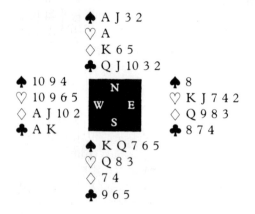

♠ A J 3 2
♥ A
♦ K 6 5
♣ Q J 10 3 2

♠ 10 9 4
♥ 10 9 6 5
♦ A J 10 2
♣ A K

♠ 8
♥ K J 7 4 2
♦ Q 9 8 3
♣ 8 7 4

♠ K Q 7 6 5
♥ Q 8 3
♦ 7 4
♣ 9 6 5

On a heart lead the play is interesting. Declarer is easily defeated if he draws three rounds of trumps. If he cashes ace and jack of trumps and then plays on clubs, he will be locked in dummy after two heart ruffs.

Suppose South tries the ace and king of trumps, then a diamond to the king and another diamond. You play a third diamond, and force in hearts each time you gain the lead in clubs. You must then come to a trump trick.

Declarer can succeed only by the double-dummy line of winning one round of trumps in dummy and then playing on clubs.

Active or Passive?

PROBLEM 5

N–S game. Match-point pairs.
Dealer North.

West holds	The bidding			
♠ A J 10 2	*W*	*N*	*E*	*S*
♡ Q 6 2		2C	—	2D
◇ K 10 5 3	—	2NT	—	3C(Baron)
♣ Q 7	—	3D	—	3H
	—	4H	all pass	

Analysis

No lead looks attractive here. North has shown a strong balanced hand with four hearts and four diamonds. South is also likely to be balanced since he initiated a Baron sequence. The objective must be to find the most passive and least dangerous lead.

The lead most likely to lose a trick is a spade. Even when North holds both spade honours, cashing the ace will save declarer a lot of work on the hand.

A lead of the queen of clubs may do no harm and could even have a deceptive effect, inducing a misguess by declarer when partner has the jack.

A diamond lead will usually work well enough when South has no honour card, although it may have the effect of providing an extra finessing entry if dummy has A Q J x.

Many players will shy away from a.trump lead with this holding, but there is no sound reason for rejecting it. The trump lead may cost a trick in the suit but declarer will often be unable to profit from this. Suppose the trump honours are split between declarer and dummy and partner has J x. When

[21]

you come in again in a side suit you will lead a second trump. Now, if declarer needs two ruffs in one hand or the other he may well refuse the finesse, allowing you to score the queen eventually. Declarer may, in fact, refuse to believe that you would lead a trump from Q x x, and your lead may generate a trump trick where none exists—for example when dummy has A K x x and declarer J 10 x x.

Marks	Small trump	10
	Queen of clubs	6
	Three of diamonds	5
	Ace of spades	2

Full hand

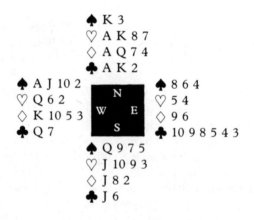

No lead defeats the contract and it is hard to say what the outcome will be, but the passive trump lead puts the defenders in a strong position to hold down the overtricks.

[22]

Active or Passive?

PROBLEM 6

Game all.
Dealer South.

Team of four.

<table>
<tr><td>West holds</td><td colspan="4">The bidding</td></tr>
<tr><td>♠ 5</td><td>W</td><td>N</td><td>E</td><td>S</td></tr>
<tr><td>♡ K 6 5 3</td><td></td><td></td><td></td><td>1S</td></tr>
<tr><td>◇ J 8 7 2</td><td>—</td><td>2C</td><td>—</td><td>3H</td></tr>
<tr><td>♣ 9 8 6 3</td><td>—</td><td>3S</td><td>—</td><td>4S</td></tr>
<tr><td></td><td colspan="2">all pass</td><td></td><td></td></tr>
</table>

Analysis

Apparently South has a strong major two-suiter. This is not an occasion for leading trumps. Apart from anything else, you would be unable to repeat the treatment when in with the king of hearts. A trump lead might damage partner's holding, and at best would concede a tempo. It seems probable that declarer will be able to establish his hearts without the aid of ruffs in dummy anyway.

There can be no case for a club lead, which would merely do declarer's work for him. It is highly likely that the jump to three hearts was based partly on some sort of club fit. If partner has tricks in clubs they will not run away.

Since a heart lead is unthinkable, you are left with the diamond suit. A forcing defence is the traditional counter when declarer has a two-suiter. South is marked with shortage in diamonds, and if you can get a force going he may be embarrassed by partner's probable four-card trump length. The normal lead of the two of diamonds may work well enough, but there could be an advantage in leading the jack. North cannot be stuffed with high diamonds since he failed to rebid three no trumps. He may have the king or queen, however, in which case the lead of the jack will enable you to hold the trick and continue the suit if declarer plays low from dummy.

Marks   Diamond jack   10
            Small diamond   5

Full hand

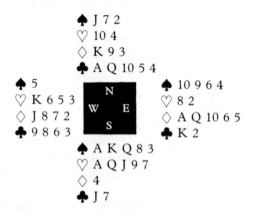

```
              ♠ J 7 2
              ♡ 10 4
              ◇ K 9 3
              ♣ A Q 10 5 4
  ♠ 5                        ♠ 10 9 6 4
  ♡ K 6 5 3        N         ♡ 8 2
  ◇ J 8 7 2    W       E     ◇ A Q 10 6 5
  ♣ 9 8 6 3        S         ♣ K 2
              ♠ A K Q 8 3
              ♡ A Q J 9 7
              ◇ 4
              ♣ J 7
```

Active or Passive?

PROBLEM 7

Game all.
Dealer South.

Team of four.

West holds

♠ 10 2
♡ 6 4 2
♢ K 7 6 3
♣ A J 10 4

The bidding

W	N	E	S
			1H
—	4C*	—	4NT
—	5D	—	6H
all pass			

* *Swiss = high-card raise to four hearts*

Analysis

The main problem is whether to make an attacking lead in one of the minors or a passive lead in a major suit.

Aggressive leading is often the right policy against small slams. In this case a diamond lead might find partner with the queen, building up a trick in the suit before the ace of clubs is driven out. However, there does not appear to be much danger of declarer discarding losing diamonds on the clubs here. The jack and ten of clubs should stop any worth-while development of the suit for declarer.

The ace of clubs would be correct only in two situations—when partner has the king of clubs and when partner has a singleton. These possibilities are distinctly remote, and in either event we might still beat the contract with a passive lead. In the first case we might come to a club and a diamond and in the second to two club tricks.

Thus neither of the attacking leads seems to be necessary. Which is the most passive lead? A trump can lose only by saving declarer a guess when partner has the doubleton queen.

More often than not partner will have a singleton trump on this auction.

A lead of the ten of spades could lose a trick in a number of situations and must therefore be relegated to second place in the markings.

Marks

A trump	10
Ten of spades	7
Ace of clubs	2
Three of diamonds	1

Full hand

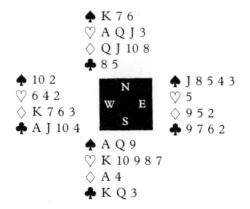

```
                    ♠ K 7 6
                    ♡ A Q J 3
                    ◇ Q J 10 8
                    ♣ 8 5
        ♠ 10 2              ♠ J 8 5 4 3
        ♡ 6 4 2      N      ♡ 5
        ◇ K 7 6 3  W   E    ◇ 9 5 2
        ♣ A J 10 4    S     ♣ 9 7 6 2
                    ♠ A Q 9
                    ♡ K 10 9 8 7
                    ◇ A 4
                    ♣ K Q 3
```

2
Listening to the Bidding

On many hands it takes a certain amount of investigation to reach a good contract. However, the auction can be most helpful to an attentive defender, enabling him to identify the enemy weakness and guiding him to the correct opening lead. This is especially true of long-winded auctions. The information available to the defenders increases in direct proportion to the number of bids made by the opponents. The obvious conclusion, which has been verified by scientific testing, is that the shortest auctions have the best chance of success.

PROBLEM 8

Game all.   Team of four.
Dealer South.

West holds	*The bidding*			
♠ K Q 8	W	N	E	S
♡ J 10 3				2C
◇ 8 6	—	2D	—	2H
♣ A Q 10 6 5	—	2NT	—	3H
	—	4H	all pass	

Analysis

Clearly if you had been partnering South you would have been able to make a lot of tricks. North and East cannot have much, and in this sort of situation it is desirable to choose as safe a lead as possible.

A club lead would be far from safe, for it is long odds that declarer has the king. A diamond lead is unlikely to give anything away, but it may take a finesse for declarer and that could be important here. Without your help declarer may have difficulty in reaching dummy to take this hypothetical finesse.

A spade lead is not without risk but it is safer than a club— there is a far better chance of finding partner with the spade jack than the club king.

But the safest lead of all is undoubtedly a trump. Which is better, an honour card or the small one? Normally you would lead the small trump to avoid crashing a singleton honour in partner's hand. But that consideration does not apply here since it is hardly possible for both North and East to have honour cards in trumps. And the lead of the three just might allow declarer easy access to dummy to take any diamond finesse that he may need.

Marks	Heart honour	10
	Heart three	8
	Spade king	6
	Diamond eight	3
	Club ace	1

Full hand

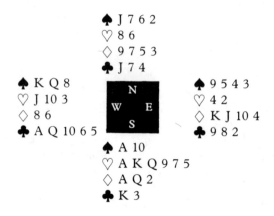

The diamond lead (and the low trump) turns out to be doubly disastrous on this hand. As well as taking a finesse for declarer it leaves West wide open to an end-play in the black suits.

PROBLEM 9

Game all.
Dealer South.

Team of four against
first-class opponents.

West holds

♠ K Q J 6
♡ 6 4
◇ K J 9 6
♣ 10 4 3

The bidding

W	N	E	S
			1S
—	2H	—	2S
—	3C	—	3S
—	4C	—	4S
all pass			

Analysis

It is comforting to hold three trump tricks behind declarer and naturally you will not be considering a spade lead.

North's bidding indicates a good two-suiter in hearts and clubs—at least 5–5 and possibly 6–5. South surely has a seven-card suit since he is missing so many spade honours, and he will have no great fit in his partner's suits. More specifically, he will not have three hearts and probably not even a strong doubleton such as K J, although he may have this sort of holding in clubs. Thus, if we consider the passive leads, a heart must be superior to a club.

Could a heart lead allow declarer to discard all his losers? It is possible. Two top hearts and three top clubs in the combined hands would be sufficient, and that is not so unlikely.

If you lead a diamond and give away a cheap trick to the queen, will it be fatal? Not necessarily. Partner should still make the ace of clubs if he has it, although he might lose the ace of hearts.

To sum up, a heart lead may be necessary when partner has the ace or king of hearts. The auction seems to indicate a weakness in diamonds, however, and an attacking diamond lead must represent the best chance for the defence.

Marks   A diamond   10
            A heart   6
            A club   2

Full hand

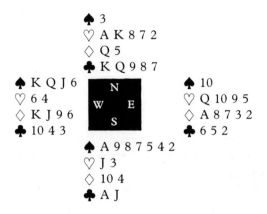

♠ 3
♡ A K 8 7 2
◊ Q 5
♣ K Q 9 8 7

♠ K Q J 6
♡ 6 4
◊ K J 9 6
♣ 10 4 3

♠ 10
♡ Q 10 9 5
◊ A 8 7 3 2
♣ 6 5 2

♠ A 9 8 7 5 4 2
♡ J 3
◊ 10 4
♣ A J

This hand is from the match between Italy and Israel in the 1975 European Championship and South was Benito Garozzo. In practice a heart was led, allowing the contract to be made.

Some experts commented that it is not enough for West to lead a diamond—he should double and lead a diamond. But not many players care to double Garozzo.

PROBLEM 10

Love all.   Team of four.
Dealer South.

West holds   *The bidding*

♠ 6 5 4   W   N   E   S
♡ K J 10 7 2   1NT(1)
♢ A 8 2   —   2NT(2)   —   3C
♣ 7 5   —   3NT(3)   —   4C(4)
                    —   5C(5)   all pass

(1) *15–17*
(2) *Transfer to 3C*
(3) *Shows 5–5 in the minors with game values*
(4) *Not happy with 3NT*
(5) *No extra values*

Analysis

The opponents are certainly armed with scientific bidding
methods. In simple terms North has indicated 5–5 in the
minors with 9–12 points, and South presumably has a
weakness in one of the majors to remove 3NT. Clearly
declarer's weak major is more likely to be hearts than spades,
and the dangerous-looking heart lead must in fact be safer
than a spade. On a spade lead there is too great a risk that
South will be able to discard dummy's losing hearts on his
good spades.

It is just possible that it is the other way round, declarer
having something like Q x x in spades and A Q x in hearts,
but the cases where a heart lead gives away a vital trick must
have a relatively low frequency.

The lead of a low diamond will work well if partner has K x

(or possibly Q x with dummy holding the king). Any doubleton diamond in partner's hand will be good enough if he has the ace of trumps, or K x x over dummy's ace.

There is little to be said for the lead of the ace of diamonds, which will be necessary only if partner has a singleton. Declarer has elected to play in clubs and it is highly unlikely that he has four diamonds as well.

A trump lead, surrendering all initiative, is unthinkable on this hand.

Marks   Heart jack (or any heart) 10
              A spade   5
              Diamond two   4
              Diamond ace   1

Full hand

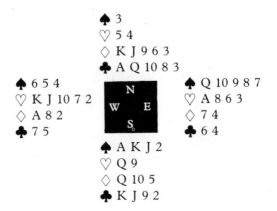

```
                    ♠ 3
                    ♡ 5 4
                    ◇ K J 9 6 3
                    ♣ A Q 10 8 3
   ♠ 6 5 4                         ♠ Q 10 9 8 7
   ♡ K J 10 7 2       N            ♡ A 8 6 3
   ◇ A 8 2        W       E        ◇ 7 4
   ♣ 7 5             S              ♣ 6 4
                    ♠ A K J 2
                    ♡ Q 9
                    ◇ Q 10 5
                    ♣ K J 9 2
```

PROBLEM 11

E–W game.   Team of four.
Dealer West.

West holds   *The bidding*

♠ A 3
♡ A K J 7 5
◇ J 3
♣ 10 8 6 2

W	*N*	*E*	*S*
1H	2NT*	—	4S
all pass			

* *"unusual", 5–5 in minors*

Analysis

Asked to choose between the minor suits, South instead
jumped to four spades. That must denote a good six- or seven-
card spade suit plus some key cards in the minors.

In defence you appear to have one trump trick and, at most,
two hearts. If partner has a trick in a minor suit it is likely to be
in diamonds, but the lead of the jack of diamonds could easily
be costly. There is not much to be said in favour of a club lead,
although it is just possible that you could give partner a
second-round club ruff. Before committing yourself to a lead
of either minor suit, however, you could cash a top heart and
look at dummy.

If you reflect on the bidding you may see a chance of
winning *three* heart tricks. Holding three small hearts, South
may be relying on his partner to control the suit. North is
known to have not more than three cards in the majors. If
these consist of one spade and two hearts, the lead of the ace of
spades would enable you to switch to hearts and try for three
tricks in the suit. The lead of a top heart would do as well for
this purpose.

[35]

But if dummy has two spades and one heart, the lead of either ace is likely to prove fatal to the defence. In this situation the only way of retaining control would be to start with your small spade. This could be costly if the diamonds are solid or if declarer has a singleton club, for he might then be able to discard a heart on one of dummy's suits. In all other cases you would be able to win the second round of trumps and try for three heart tricks. On balance, this seems to offer the best chance of defeating the contract.

Marks	Spade three	10
	Heart ace or king	6
	Spade ace	3

Full hand

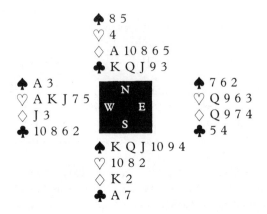

Note that the underlead of the ace of spades will not necessarily fail when North has a singleton spade and two hearts.

PROBLEM 12

Game all.   Match-point pairs.
Dealer South.

West holds   *The bidding*

♠ 7 6   *W   N   E   S*
♡ A 10 8 6 3   1S
◇ K Q 2   —   2H —   3H
♣ 10 7 4   —   3S —   4S
                           all pass

Analysis

The bidding has been informative. North should have five hearts for his response of two hearts and South three for his raise, so you can be certain of giving partner at least one heart ruff. You could start with the ace of hearts, for instance, and continue with the ten of hearts as a suit-preference signal asking for a diamond return. However, this is likely to work well only if partner has the ace of diamonds or the ace of trumps. Otherwise, declarer will win the diamond switch, draw trumps, and discard a couple of minor-suit losers on the long hearts.

To realise the full defensive potential of the hand, you must give partner his ruff before releasing the ace of hearts. Lead the ten of hearts at trick one (not a low one, for you do not want a club return). Partner will ruff and switch to diamonds, and you will score the tricks that are due to you in the minor suits since you still have control of the hearts.

Of the other leads, the king of diamonds at least has the merit of setting up a probable trick or two in diamonds, but that may not be enough to give you a good score. Nothing else is worth considering.

Marks

Heart ten	10
Heart ace	5
Low heart	3
Diamond king	2

Full hand

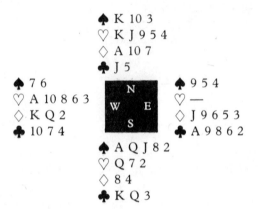

```
                    ♠ K 10 3
                    ♡ K J 9 5 4
                    ◇ A 10 7
                    ♣ J 5
   ♠ 7 6                          ♠ 9 5 4
   ♡ A 10 8 6 3        N          ♡ —
   ◇ K Q 2         W       E      ◇ J 9 6 5 3
   ♣ 10 7 4            S          ♣ A 9 8 6 2
                    ♠ A Q J 8 2
                    ♡ Q 7 2
                    ◇ 8 4
                    ♣ K Q 3
```

PROBLEM 13

E–W game.   Team of four.
Dealer East.

West holds   *The bidding*

♠ 8 2 | W | N | E | S |
♡ A 8 7 2 | --- | --- | --- | --- |
◇ 10 9 5 | | | — | 1S |
♣ J 9 6 3 | — | 2D | — | 3C |
                             | — | 4S | — | 5C |
                             | — | 5D | — | 5S |
                             | all pass |

Analysis

The bidding indicates strong hands on either side of you. Each opponent in turn made a slam try, yet they have subsided at the five-level. Clearly neither of them has a heart control, and the heart suit is the obvious place to look for defensive tricks.

There are certainly two heart tricks to cash since partner is marked with the king, and it may even be possible to score three hearts to defeat the contract. If each opponent has three cards in the suit and North or East has the queen, the lead of the ace will enable you to win three tricks whenever they are winnable. But if the queen is in the South hand, the only lead to give you a chance of three tricks is a low heart.

Normally it is dangerous to underlead an ace against a high-level contract, but here there is no risk at all. Partner knows from the bidding that you have the ace, and he knows that you know he has the king. A further point is that it is not impossible for North to have four hearts and East the king doubleton, in which case the underlead is the only way for the defenders to make three tricks.

Marks   Heart two   10
           Heart ace   5

Full hand

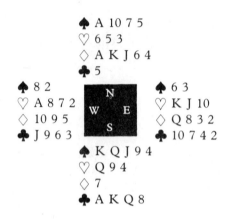

```
                    ♠ A 10 7 5
                    ♡ 6 5 3
                    ◇ A K J 6 4
                    ♣ 5
    ♠ 8 2              N              ♠ 6 3
    ♡ A 8 7 2      W     E           ♡ K J 10
    ◇ 10 9 5                         ◇ Q 8 3 2
    ♣ J 9 6 3         S              ♣ 10 7 4 2
                    ♠ K Q J 9 4
                    ♡ Q 9 4
                    ◇ 7
                    ♣ A K Q 8
```

PROBLEM 14

Game all.   Team of four.
Dealer East.

West holds   *The bidding*

♠ 10 7 6 2   W   N   E   S
♡ A 10 5   3H   4C*
♢ Q 10 3   4H   4S   —   6C
♣ A 9 6   all pass

                                 * *for takeout*

Analysis

South presumably has a strong minor two-suiter and was prepared to hear preference to diamonds at the six-level. There can be little point in leading the ace of hearts, for it is hardly conceivable that South would jump to six clubs, missing the ace of trumps, without a heart void. His distribution is likely to be 1–0–6–6, 2–0–6–5 or 2–0–5–6.

The question is, will declarer be able to ruff a diamond in dummy? If so, the ace and another club may be the best defence. This is not likely to be effective when dummy has more than two clubs, however, for declarer probably needs only one diamond ruff to establish the suit. It is hard to imagine that the lead of a small club could ever be right.

Alternatively, you could take the view that the possibility of discards on dummy's spade suit is a more serious threat than that of a diamond ruff on the table. By leading a spade initially and a second spade when in with the ace of clubs, you can cut dummy adrift and hope eventually to score a diamond trick. This defence will also work in those cases where South has two spades and North is 2–2 in the minors. North must then have a six-card spade suit and you will be able to give partner a second-round ruff. All things considered, the spade attack seems more likely to succeed than trump leads.

Marks   Spade   10
           Club ace   7
           Heart ace   1

Full hand

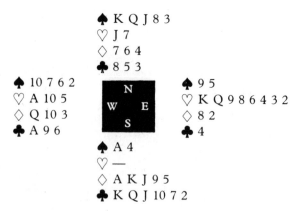

♠ K Q J 8 3
♥ J 7
♦ 7 6 4
♣ 8 5 3

♠ 10 7 6 2
♥ A 10 5
♦ Q 10 3
♣ A 9 6

♠ 9 5
♥ K Q 9 8 6 4 3 2
♦ 8 2
♣ 4

♠ A 4
♥ —
♦ A K J 9 5
♣ K Q J 10 7 2

3
"Blind" Leads against No Trumps

A defender has little to guide him when the bidding goes—one no trump, three no trumps. Still, even in such an uninformative auction, negative inferences can be drawn from the fact that the opponents failed to bid a major suit and failed to use Stayman. If the decision is close, this may tip the scales in favour of a major-suit lead.

In general a defender will not go far wrong in leading the fourth-highest card of his longest and strongest suit. From certain honour combinations, however, the right choice of card is not always obvious.

PROBLEM 15

Game all.   Team of four.
Dealer South.

West holds   *The bidding*

♠ 8 7 2   W   N   E   S
♡ A Q J 4 2   1NT(16–18)
◇ 7 6 3   —   3NT   all pass
♣ 8 2

Analysis

You require no help from the bidding here, for the cards in your own hand make it clear that the heart suit offers by far the best chance of defeating the contract. It must be right to attack the suit yourself rather than lead something else in the hope that partner can twice gain the lead to push hearts through. The real problem is whether to lead the queen or a small card.

The small card will be superior (a) when partner has a doubleton king and the suit is divided 4–2 between the opponents, (b) when partner has a small doubleton and either declarer or dummy has a doubleton king, and (c) when partner has a doubleton ten and declarer has K x x x. In the latter case declarer may go wrong by winning the first trick; whatever happens, you will be better placed than if you had led the queen.

The lead of the queen will gain when dummy has three cards headed by the king and declarer a doubleton, with the ten in either hand. It will also save a trick when dummy has K x x and declarer 10 x x, although in this case you can never establish the heart suit. It appears that the lead of the small heart has a definite edge.

[45]

Of the other suits a spade is the best choice. It is normal to prefer a trebleton to a doubleton and a major to a minor.

Marks		
	Heart four	10
	Heart queen	7
	Spade	4
	Diamond	2
	Club	1

Full hand

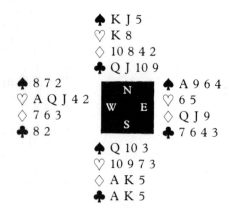

♠ K J 5
♥ K 8
♦ 10 8 4 2
♣ Q J 10 9

♠ 8 7 2
♥ A Q J 4 2
♦ 7 6 3
♣ 8 2

♠ A 9 6 4
♥ 6 5
♦ Q J 9
♣ 7 6 4 3

♠ Q 10 3
♥ 10 9 7 3
♦ A K 5
♣ A K 5

PROBLEM 16

E–W game.   Team of four.
Dealer South.

West holds   *The bidding*

♠ K 9 6
♡ Q 8 7 6 3
♢ Q 6 4 3
♣ 3

W	N	E	S
			1C
—	1D	—	2H
—	3C	—	3D
—	3S	—	3NT
all pass			

Analysis

South's bidding indicates a 1–4–3–5 shape with about 20 high-card points. His singleton spade is likely to be an honour card. Possible spade holdings in the North hand are J 10 x, 10 8 x x, J x x x or Q x x.

North must be short in hearts, but the moderate quality of your suit is not encouraging. You would need to find partner with several heart honours to make the lead worth while.

On this bidding there is really no need to look beyond the spade suit. Partner is marked with at least five spades, which makes this the natural point of attack. The question is, which card should you lead? The king may be necessary if declarer has a singleton queen or jack, but this lead will be damaging to the defence when declarer has a singleton ace.

There is little to choose between the nine and the six of spades; theoretically the nine is better in case dummy has Q 10 x x opposite the singleton eight, but this is perhaps rather unlikely.

On balance the spectacular lead of the spade king seems to offer the best chance.

Marks	Spade king	10
	Spade nine	8
	Spade six	7
	Heart six	2

Full hand

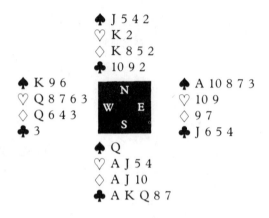

```
                ♠ J 5 4 2
                ♡ K 2
                ◇ K 8 5 2
                ♣ 10 9 2
♠ K 9 6                          ♠ A 10 8 7 3
♡ Q 8 7 6 3         N            ♡ 10 9
◇ Q 6 4 3       W       E        ◇ 9 7
♣ 3                 S            ♣ J 6 5 4
                ♠ Q
                ♡ A J 5 4
                ◇ A J 10
                ♣ A K Q 8 7
```

"Blind" Leads against No Trumps

PROBLEM 17

Love all.   Team of four.
Dealer North.

West holds   *The bidding*

♠ 7 6
♡ A 2
♢ 8 7 6 5
♣ A Q 10 3 2

W	N	E	S
	1C(1)	—	1NT(2)
—	2C(3)	—	2D(4)
—	2H(5)	—	2NT(6)
—	3NT	all pass	

(1) *Precision, 16 + points*
(2) *Balanced 8–13 points*
(3) *Stayman-type enquiry*
(4) *8–10 with four hearts*
(5) *Further enquiry*
(6) *3–4–3–3 shape*

Analysis

You have an accurate picture of declarer's shape and strength but you do not know where his honour cards are located. As for North's hand you can only infer: he will not be too unbalanced in view of his enquiry bid, he will not have five spades or he would have bid the suit, but he is likely to have four spades since he continued the enquiry. All this indicates that there is no reason to consider any suit other than clubs, and there are three possible leads.

A small club. This will be helpful if partner has the singleton king, or even the singleton jack. Alternatively, dummy may have a doubleton king. The small club lead will also be best when declarer has the king, with the jack either in the North or the South hand. You will need to find partner with an entry, which is not impossible. However, it will have to be a quick entry such as an ace. If partner has a couple of queens, declarer will take any two-way finesses into your hand in order to protect his club holding, and that is just what you do not want. The small club lead would have more going for it if the opponents' clubs could be divided 4–2, but you know from the bidding that South has three clubs.

Queen of clubs. This could get your name in the papers! The strong hand is on your left, so there is a fair chance of finding K x x in dummy opposite J x x. But you will still need to find partner with a quick entry, which must be against the odds. The queen lead will also work when dummy has the doubleton jack, of course.

Ace of clubs. This lead is likely to bring instant success or failure. Its main attraction is that if you find dummy with either K x or J x you can virtually guarantee to defeat the contract without more than marginal help from partner.

Marks	Ace of clubs	10
	Three of clubs	9
	Queen of clubs	7

Full hand

```
                    ♠ K J 10 2
                    ♡ K Q
                    ◇ K Q 9 3
                    ♣ K 7 5
  ♠ 7 6                           ♠ A 8 5 4
  ♡ A 2            N              ♡ 9 8 7 6 5
  ◇ 8 7 6 5    W       E          ◇ 10 2
  ♣ A Q 10 3 2     S              ♣ 6 4
                    ♠ Q 9 3
                    ♡ J 10 4 3
                    ◇ A J 4
                    ♣ J 9 8
```

As you can see, the lead of the queen of clubs works best in this particular case. Still, if you start with the ace you can recover by finding the right switch and getting a club return from partner. Even if you switch to a diamond, declarer may tackle his major suits in the wrong order. And if he guesses right, leading a heart to knock out your ace? Well, you can't win them all.

PROBLEM 18

E–W game.   Team of four.
Dealer North.

West holds	*The bidding*			
♠ Q 10 4	W	N	E	S
♡ K Q J 3		1H	—	2C
◇ 8 6 5	—	2D	—	3NT
♣ A K 6	all pass			

Analysis

A glance at your picture gallery tells you that partner can have little in the way of high cards. There is no point in leading your low spade even if partner has the jack. Declarer must have seven top tricks—the ace and king of spades, four diamonds and the ace of hearts—and he will surely be able to develop two more tricks in clubs before you can set up five tricks for the defence. A lead of the queen or ten of spades could be the winning move when partner has five spades headed by the jack, however. If declarer holds up on the first or second round of spades you can switch to hearts.

What about a heart lead? The king of hearts would work well in situations where declarer has the singleton ten opposite A 8 x x x, but the queen of hearts would do the same job and has the advantage of an element of deception. With singleton ten opposite A 9 7 x x, for instance, declarer might misguess on the second round.

However, the opening lead of the three of hearts is even more deceptive, for it may allow partner to score the nine over dummy's A 10 8 x x. Furthermore, there is no reason why partner should not have the singleton ten of hearts. The low heart lead will not necessarily fail when dummy has A 10 9 x x. If declarer fears a spade switch he may go up with the ace of hearts, hoping to drop an honour from East.

Marks	Heart three	10
	Heart queen	7
	Heart king	4
	Spade queen or ten	3

Full hand

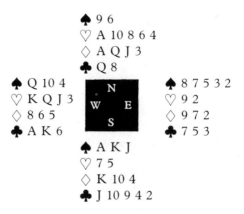

```
              ♠ 9 6
              ♡ A 10 8 6 4
              ◇ A Q J 3
              ♣ Q 8
♠ Q 10 4                    ♠ 8 7 5 3 2
♡ K Q J 3         N         ♡ 9 2
◇ 8 6 5        W     E      ◇ 9 7 2
♣ A K 6           S         ♣ 7 5 3
              ♠ A K J
              ♡ 7 5
              ◇ K 10 4
              ♣ J 10 9 4 2
```

This is the right occasion for a deceptive lead—when you know partner to be so weak that it will not matter if he is deceived. The dangerous time for deception is when you expect partner to win a trick or two in defence. He may then be deceived into making a fatal switch.

PROBLEM 19

Game all. Team of four.
Dealer North.

West holds	*The bidding*			
♠ A J 8 3	W	N	E	S
♡ 6 5		3D	—	3NT
◇ 5 4	all pass			
♣ A Q 7 5 3				

Analysis

Your strong holdings in the black suits make it appear virtually certain that declarer will have a fit in diamonds and that he will be able to run seven tricks in the suit.

The lead of a low card in either spades or clubs runs the obvious risk of giving declarer a cheap trick in the suit. That, with the ace of hearts and seven diamonds, would see him home. Nor is a heart lead any better; declarer could just as easily make his contract with two hearts and seven diamonds.

In situations like this the lead of an ace is almost mandatory—it gives you the best chance of running either black suit when this is possible.

Of the two aces the club ace has a definite edge. It will rarely cost when partner has the king, whereas the lead of the spade ace may be catastrophic when partner has the king without the queen. To put it another way, when you start with the ace of clubs you retain the chance of running the clubs or switching successfully to a low spade (that eight of spades could be an important card if partner has K 10 x and dummy 9 x). But if you start with the ace of spades and find that you have only two tricks in the suit, the chances of a successful switch are less bright.

Marks

Club ace		10
Spade ace		6
Small club		2
Small spade		2
Heart		1

Full hand

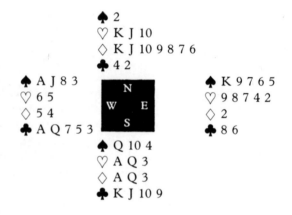

```
                    ♠ 2
                    ♡ K J 10
                    ◇ K J 10 9 8 7 6
                    ♣ 4 2
    ♠ A J 8 3                       ♠ K 9 7 6 5
    ♡ 6 5              N            ♡ 9 8 7 4 2
    ◇ 5 4          W     E          ◇ 2
    ♣ A Q 7 5 3       S            ♣ 8 6
                    ♠ Q 10 4
                    ♡ A Q 3
                    ◇ A Q 3
                    ♣ K J 10 9
```

When partner plays a discouraging six on your ace of clubs you switch to the three of spades. On winning with the king, how does East know to return a spade rather than a club? The answer lies in the size of your spade. The three of spades indicated values in the suit and asked for a spade return. Had you wanted a club return you would have led a higher spade, the eight, perhaps, to express lack of interest in spades. This is known as attitude signalling and is widely used by good players.

PROBLEM 20

Game all.   Team of four.
Dealer South.

West holds	*The bidding*		

	W	*N*	*E*	*S*
♠ 10 4 2				2NT*
♡ K Q 8 6 3				
◇ 9 2	—	3C**	—	3D
♣ 8 7 3	—	3NT	all pass	
	* 21–22		** Stayman	

Analysis

North presumably has a major suit which is likely to be spades. The defence may be able to run five tricks in hearts, which is a cogent argument in favour of leading your fourth-highest heart.

Of the short suit leads a spade must be the worst. There is little to choose between diamonds and clubs, although in general a trebleton should be preferred to a doubleton.

Is there any point in leading a heart other than the six—perhaps a deceptive three? Very little in this case. The time for that is when you hold most of the likely entries.

Is there a case for the king of hearts? This could obviously be the right move when declarer has A J doubleton opposite a doubleton or a worthless trebleton. A more subtle case is where declarer has A J opposite 10 x x or the equivalent. Whatever you lead you have a chance of establishing the suit, but the lead of the king gains a tempo. An even more valuable tempo may be gained when declarer has something like A J x opposite 10 x. If declarer wins the first trick he gives you the chance to get the suit going, and if he holds up he gives you an opportunity to judge the best switch.

[55]

On the other side of the coin, the lead of the king is likely to cost a trick when dummy has four hearts, although this is probably a hopeless situation for the defence even if a small heart is led. Also, the lead of the king will lose when declarer has A x opposite J 9 x, a situation in which he is likely to misguess if a small heart is led. The major disadvantage of leading the king, however, is that it strangles the defence when partner has the doubleton ace.

Thus there are strong arguments both for and against the lead of the king of hearts—perhaps the cons just outweigh the pros.

Marks		
	Heart six	10
	Heart king	8
	Heart three	2
	Club eight	2
	Diamond nine	1

Full hand

```
                    ♠ J 9 8 3
                    ♡ 10 5
                    ◇ Q J 10 3
                    ♣ 6 5 4
     ♠ 10 4 2          N          ♠ Q 7 6
     ♡ K Q 8 6 3    W     E       ♡ 9 4 2
     ◇ 9 2             S          ◇ A 8 4
     ♣ 8 7 3                      ♣ A 10 9 2
                    ♠ A K 5
                    ♡ A J 7
                    ◇ K 7 6 5
                    ♣ K Q J
```

The layout above is one which rewards the lead of the king of hearts rather than the six. If the king is taken, the defenders make five tricks—three hearts and two aces. If the king of hearts is allowed to win, a club switch and accurate defence still beat the contract.

PROBLEM 21

N–S game.   Team of four.
Dealer North.

West holds   *The bidding*

♠ A J 9 5   *W*   *N*   *E*   *S*
♡ A Q J   1H   —   2C
♢ K 10 4 2   —   2H   —   3NT
♣ 9 5   all pass

Analysis

Normally, when there is a choice between two unbid suits, the winning strategy is to try to develop tricks in the suit that is not headed by an ace. But things are far from normal here. You have 15 points and declarer has bid strongly, so it must be highly unlikely that partner has as much as a queen in his hand. A diamond lead is therefore unattractive because of the heavy risk of presenting declarer with a cheap trick. Partner just might have the jack of diamonds with length in the suit, of course. If you decide that you must attack in diamonds there is a good case for leading the king, hoping to pin a singleton queen in dummy.

But the better shot must be to play partner for length in spades, aiming to defeat the contract with four spade tricks and the ace of hearts. A lead of the five of spades is not likely to succeed unless partner, with 10 x x x x, has the perspicacity to hang on to his ten. A lead of the jack or nine of spades, on the other hand, will work even when partner has five small spades if both declarer and dummy have doubletons. However, you can do better than that. The lead of the ace of spades will cope just as well with these situations, and it will also cater for the

cases where dummy has a singleton king or queen and partner
has 10 x x x x.

Marks

Spade ace	10
Spade jack or nine	7
Spade five	3
Diamond king	2
Small diamond	1

Full hand

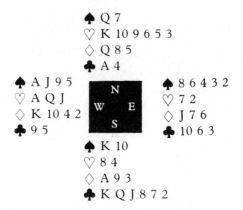

```
                 ♠ Q 7
                 ♡ K 10 9 6 5 3
                 ◇ Q 8 5
                 ♣ A 4
  ♠ A J 9 5                        ♠ 8 6 4 3 2
  ♡ A Q J          N              ♡ 7 2
  ◇ K 10 4 2    W     E           ◇ J 7 6
  ♣ 9 5            S              ♣ 10 6 3
                 ♠ K 10
                 ♡ 8 4
                 ◇ A 9 3
                 ♣ K Q J 8 7 2
```

4

Help from Partner

It should be a little easier to find the best lead when partner has been active in the bidding. If partner has bid a suit, for instance, it will usually be a good idea to lead his suit. A third-in-hand bid, in particular, may have been made with the sole purpose of indicating a good lead. However, the lead of partner's suit should not be allowed to become an automatic reflex. As always, each situation must be considered on its merits.

A double from partner can also be highly informative. Some doubles are made with the intention of extracting a penalty, others for the purpose of indicating the winning defence. Used in the latter sense, the double can be a potent weapon indeed.

PROBLEM 22

N–S game.　　　　　　Team of four.
Dealer East.

West holds		*The bidding*			
♠ Q 10 6 5 2		W	N	E	S
♡ 10 9 3				1S	2D
◇ 6		2S	5D	all pass	
♣ Q 8 5 4					

Analysis

On this bidding there will not be more than one spade trick for the defence, which leaves two further tricks to be found. Partner will have some high cards in at least one of the side suits, and in order to score these cards he may need a lead from you through dummy. For this reason the initial lead of a low spade would not be a good idea. The chance to push a side suit through dummy would have gone, for you would be unlikely ever to regain the lead.

There is something to be said for the lead of either a heart or a club initially. Of the two the heart lead is less likely to give away a trick, but here you are concerned not so much with safety as with the need to develop fast tricks for the defence. From that point of view the two suits are about equal. It's just a guessing game.

It would help to eliminate guesswork if you could have a look at dummy first, and there is a good chance of doing that if you start with the queen of spades. With any luck the queen will hold the trick and you will be in a position to make an informed decision about your switch.

Marks	Spade queen	10
	Heart ten	5
	Low club	5
	Low spade	2

Full hand

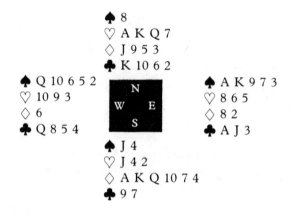

In this case it is a club switch that is required, but it might equally well have been a heart.

PROBLEM 23

N–S game.   Team of four.
Dealer East.

West holds   *The bidding*

♠ A 5
♡ J 9 8 7 5 3
◇ J 3
♣ Q 10 4

W	N	E	S
			3D	3S
—	4S	Dbl	all pass

Analysis

What is going on? East has opened with a non-vulnerable pre-emptive bid of three diamonds yet has doubled the opponents in game without hearing a peep from you. How can he have the strength to do that? Your trumps show that there can be no bad trump break, and this must be obvious to East as well.

There can be only one logical explanation. East has doubled not because he is confident of defeating four spades but in order to indicate the only defence that *might* succeed. He is asking you not to lead a diamond but to give him a ruff in a side suit.

If East has a void it is long odds that it is in hearts. Now you have to consider the suit-preference implications of the card you lead. A low heart would ask for a club return, a high heart for a diamond. There is no way to request a trump return.

Although the chance of scoring a club trick cannot be bright, you certainly do not want to encourage a diamond return. The lead of a high heart might even persuade partner to make a disastrous underlead of the ace of diamonds at the next trick. Since you will still have trump control, the

[63]

diamonds can wait. The three of hearts is the correct lead.

Marks   Heart three   10
           Anything else   0

Full hand

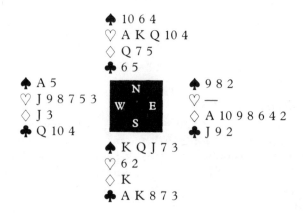

East's imaginative double paves the way for the defeat of a contract that would otherwise be made. You have to be careful not to spoil things by leading a high heart.

PROBLEM 24

E–W game.   Team of four.
Dealer West.

West holds   *The bidding*

	W	N	E	S
♠ 7	—	1D	1S	1NT
♡ 10 5 4	—	2D	2H	2S
◇ 9 8 2	—	3C	—	3NT
♣ A 10 8 7 4 3	—	—	Dbl	all pass

Analysis

The double in this situation traditionally calls for the lead of partner's first-bid suit, but let us analyse further. North has shown 6–4 distribution in diamonds and clubs and must have at least one heart, since South, who is in the upper range for his one no trump response, would surely have doubled two hearts if he had length in the suit. South must therefore have at least four and quite possibly five spades. Yet in spite of this spade length South did not double one spade for penalties at an attractive vulnerability. The reason can only be that his spades are not too strong.

This analysis seems to support the traditional interpretation of the double. East will either have a running spade suit or, more likely, a suit with a gap plus a diamond trick. Further confirmation is provided by a study of your own heart holding; the presence of the ten of hearts proves that partner cannot have a heart suit with only one gap. The singleton spade is therefore the indicated lead.

A case can be made for leading the ace of clubs to have a look at dummy. This is unlikely to give declarer the contract, but it may reduce the penalty.

Marks   Seven of spades   10
           Ace of clubs   4

Full hand

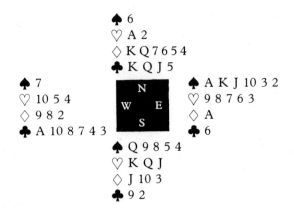

Some partnerships like to attach a firm meaning to this sort of double of three no trumps, others prefer to keep a free hand and work things out at the table.

PROBLEM 25

Game all.   Team of four.
Dealer East.

West holds   *The bidding*

♠ A Q   W   N   E   S
♡ 8 5   3S   4H
♢ A Q 6 5 4   4S   5H   all pass
♣ 8 7 3 2

Analysis

At this vulnerability partner almost certainly has the spade king, so a lead of the ace of spades is unlikely to give anything away. It will enable you to have a look at dummy and decide on the best defence.

A trump lead would serve no purpose and would be positively dangerous—declarer may be able to run seven hearts and four clubs if you let him in. A club lead will help only in the remote situation where partner has a void. If East has a natural club trick you are likely to beat the contract on any lead.

The ace of diamonds is not an attractive lead. Even if partner has a singleton or void in diamonds you will still need a trick from spades. Nothing can be lost (expect perhaps an extra undertrick) by starting with the spade suit.

The lead that covers nearly all possibilities is the queen of spades. This also caters for the common situations where you have only one spade trick and a diamond lead from partner is required. Of course, partner will need to be sufficiently awake to cover the queen of spades with his king.

Marks   Spade queen   10
              Spade ace   4
              Club   1
              Diamond ace   1

Full hand

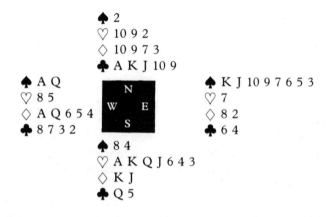

♠ 2
♡ 10 9 2
◇ 10 9 7 3
♣ A K J 10 9

♠ A Q
♡ 8 5
◇ A Q 6 5 4
♣ 8 7 3 2

♠ K J 10 9 7 6 5 3
♡ 7
◇ 8 2
♣ 6 4

♠ 8 4
♡ A K Q J 6 4 3
◇ K J
♣ Q 5

East is fortunate enough to have K J 10 9 in spades which makes it relatively easy to overtake the queen. He would be more severely tested if the jack of spades were with South.

PROBLEM 26

N–S game.   Match-point pairs.
Dealer North.

West holds   *The bidding*

♠ K J 6 5 3   W   N   E   S
♡ 7   1C   1S   2H
♢ 8 5 3 2   4S   5H   Dbl all pass
♣ 7 6 4

Analysis

In this situation East must have a sound double and high hopes of defeating the contract. He would not dissipate all the advantage of having pushed the opponents to the five-level and risk the loss of 850 by making a dubious double.

If you are thinking about a spade lead, the king is theoretically better than a small card, but can a spade lead be right at all? Partner is not likely to be counting on the ace of spades as a trick after this auction. He probably has three outside winners including a stopper in one of the enemy suits—hearts or clubs. Partner can be relied on for one trick or more in diamonds, and a diamond is surely the correct lead.

There is little chance of giving partner a ruff in clubs, for with a void in clubs he would surely have pressed on to five spades. However, a club lead may enable East to cash his winners and is therefore better than a spade.

Marks   A diamond   10
             A club   3
             Spade king   1

Full hand

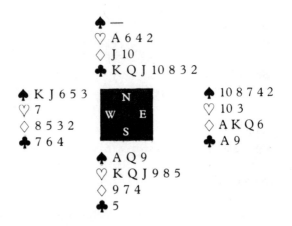

```
                    ♠ —
                    ♡ A 6 4 2
                    ◇ J 10
                    ♣ K Q J 10 8 3 2
    ♠ K J 6 5 3                      ♠ 10 8 7 4 2
    ♡ 7              N               ♡ 10 3
    ◇ 8 5 3 2     W     E            ◇ A K Q 6
    ♣ 7 6 4          S               ♣ A 9
                    ♠ A Q 9
                    ♡ K Q J 9 8 5
                    ◇ 9 7 4
                    ♣ 5
```

This hand comes from the English Life Masters Pairs of 1969. By doubling, the East players hoped to avert a spade lead.

However, the South players who notched up 1050 for five hearts doubled with an overtrick had to be content with 12 match-points out of 20. The auction was common and so was the spade lead!

PROBLEM 27

Game all.   Team of four.
Dealer South.

West holds	*The bidding*			
♠ Q 5 4	*W*	*N*	*E*	*S*
♡ 9 7 5				—
◇ K J 9 4	—	1S	2C	2H
♣ 5 4 3	—	3H	—	3NT
	—	4H	all pass	

Analysis

North's heart raise appears to have been based on distribution rather than high cards. South must be near the maximum for his initial pass, and he is likely to have a double stopper in clubs in view of his attempt to play in three no trumps. Partner will have a good suit, almost certainly six cards in length, with some outside high cards.

You need powerful reasons to reject a lead of partner's suit, but here the indications are strong enough. North can hardly have more than one card in the suit, and a club lead will make it easy for declarer to discard losing diamonds from dummy on his club honours.

A diamond lead must give the defence a better chance. This may give away a trick, but the risk is well worth taking. In fact partner is likely to have a high card in diamonds, since his club suit has a couple of gaps and he cannot have much in hearts or spades.

A trump lead is not likely to achieve much. Although the opponents have not shown overwhelming strength, there are several bad signs for the defence. Suits appear to be breaking evenly with the cards well placed for declarer, and this argues against a passive defence.

Marks	Diamond four	10
	A club	5
	A trump	1

Full hand

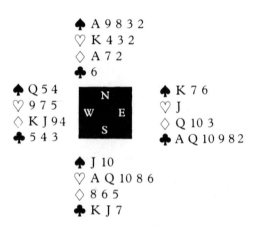

```
              ♠ A 9 8 3 2
              ♡ K 4 3 2
              ◇ A 7 2
              ♣ 6
  ♠ Q 5 4                    ♠ K 7 6
  ♡ 9 7 5        N           ♡ J
  ◇ K J 9 4   W     E        ◇ Q 10 3
  ♣ 5 4 3        S           ♣ A Q 10 9 8 2
              ♠ J 10
              ♡ A Q 10 8 6
              ◇ 8 6 5
              ♣ K J 7
```

The irony of the hand is that three no trumps cannot be beaten as the cards lie. However, if South had bid a direct four hearts instead of three no trumps, a club would have been led and the heart game would have been made.

PROBLEM 28

N–S game.   Team of four.
Dealer East.

West holds	*The bidding*			
♠ 8 7	*W*	*N*	*E*	*S*
♡ J 7 2			1H	Dbl
◇ 10 9 2	—	2H	3H	3S
♣ K 9 8 6 5	—	4NT	—	5C
	—	6S	Dbl	all pass

Analysis

Partner's double asks for a non-heart lead—presumably he is void in either clubs or diamonds. Since you have five clubs and only three diamonds, it seems likely that partner's void will be in clubs, but it may be as well to look more deeply into the auction.

You have four points and partner will have at least ten. Give South twelve for his takeout double, and that leaves North with fourteen points on which he has driven to a slam. He must have very good distribution—probably four spades and a six-card minor.

If South has a minimum double his hand will be suitable in other respects—singleton or void heart with support for the other suits, at least three cards in each of them. North's long minor and South's supporting cards will therefore make up a total of at least nine cards. If this analysis is correct, North's long minor cannot be clubs and partner would appear to have a diamond void.

Besides indicating a void, does partner's double guarantee a side ace or not? This is largely a matter of partnership style. If you play that partner must have a cashing trick, the king of clubs is a good lead. When partner has the ace you will hold the first trick and give him a diamond ruff. And if the preceding arguments are wrong and partner is void in clubs after all, he can ruff the king of clubs and cash his diamond ace.

Marks	A diamond	10
	King of clubs	10
	Small club	2

Full hand

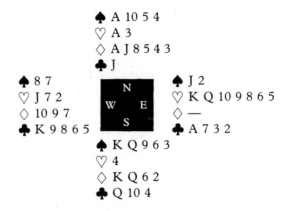

```
                    ♠ A 10 5 4
                    ♡ A 3
                    ◇ A J 8 5 4 3
                    ♣ J
      ♠ 8 7             N          ♠ J 2
      ♡ J 7 2        W     E       ♡ K Q 10 9 8 6 5
      ◇ 10 9 7          S          ◇ —
      ♣ K 9 8 6 5                  ♣ A 7 3 2
                    ♠ K Q 9 6 3
                    ♡ 4
                    ◇ K Q 6 2
                    ♣ Q 10 4
```

This hand came up in a match between the Aces and the Omar Sharif Bridge Circus. At both tables a small club was led against six spades doubled, which only goes to show that it is a difficult problem.

PROBLEM 29

Game all.   Team of four.
Dealer East.

West holds   *The bidding*

♠ A 6 5 4

W	N	E	S
		3C	4C*
5C	—	—	5H
all pass			

♡ 7 6 5 4
◇ 8 6
♣ A 5 4

* *strong two-suiter with any two suits*

Analysis

Your holding suggests diamonds as South's second suit but the auction favours spades. With equal length in his suits South would normally bid the lower-ranking one first.

If South has spades partner may have a singleton, in which case you can give him a second-round ruff. However, the defence will still need a third trick, and it is hard to see where that might come from unless you have a club to cash, so you might as well start with a club. A spade lead could be damaging to the defence if declarer's second suit is diamonds. And there can be little point in a diamond lead.

A club lead strikes a nice balance between safety and aggression, giving nothing away while offering prospects of a forcing defence. Even if declarer is void in clubs, you will be in with a chance when partner has a trick in declarer's second suit. If you lead the ace of clubs and dummy goes down with something like Q x x in the suit, *you* will need to win the first side-suit trick to keep the force going. But there will be no profitable way of doing this if partner has the singleton king of spades.

This suggests an underlead of the ace of clubs at trick one to keep the defence more flexible. There is little risk, for if dummy has K x x declarer is unlikely to put up the king. Now you can allow East to win the first spade and a club return will keep up the force. The low club lead also caters for the situation where you have a cashing club trick and East has a small singleton spade.

Marks	Small club	10
	Ace of clubs	9
	Ace of spades	2
	Diamond eight	1

Full hand

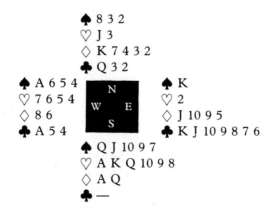

```
              ♠ 8 3 2
              ♡ J 3
              ◇ K 7 4 3 2
              ♣ Q 3 2
   ♠ A 6 5 4         ♠ K
   ♡ 7 6 5 4    N    ♡ 2
   ◇ 8 6      W   E  ◇ J 10 9 5
   ♣ A 5 4      S    ♣ K J 10 9 8 7 6
              ♠ Q J 10 9 7
              ♡ A K Q 10 9 8
              ◇ A Q
              ♣ —
```

The lead of a small club puts the defence in a strong position. Declarer can still make his contract if he plays for a 4–1 trump split, cashing just one trump and then playing on spades, but in practice he is likely to go down.

5

Leading against Part-Scores

Low-level contracts can be difficult to defend against. The defenders need to win five or more tricks, and at the outset it can be hard to see where all the tricks might come from. However, there is often a little more latitude in the defence. When a contract is beatable there may be more than one way of beating it, and there is a better chance of recovering from an unlucky choice of lead.

PROBLEM 30

Love all.   Rubber bridge
Dealer North.

West holds	*The bidding*			
♠ Q J 2	W	N	E	S
♡ K Q 2		—	—	1C
◇ J 8 6	—	—	Dbl	—
♣ Q 7 6 5	1NT	2C	all pass	

Analysis

North is marked with a weak hand containing four or five
clubs and a probable ruffing value. Of the attacking side-suit
leads, the queen of spades seems an obvious first choice.
Holdings such as K 10 x or A 10 x in spades are unlikely in a
dummy that is known to be weak, hence the spade lead is
reasonably safe. The same cannot be said for a heart lead since
dummy could well have the jack of hearts and declarer the ace.
And a diamond is not too attractive from J 8 6.

A trump lead would be passive and might help to cut down
ruffs in dummy. With several potential entry cards, you
should have the chance to continue the trump attack if this
appears desirable. You would have to sacrifice your trump
trick to do this, but in such cases the trick often comes back
with interest.

There could be an advantage in having the first trump lead
come from partner, although he can have no more than a
singleton. A spade lead might enable partner to gain the lead
and push his trump through declarer. Then you could play a
second round of trumps from your hand without giving up
your trump trick.

[79]

The decision seems finely balanced between a trump and the queen of spades, with the other leads a long way behind.

Marks	Low trump	10
	Spade queen	9
	Heart king	3
	Diamond six	2

Full hand

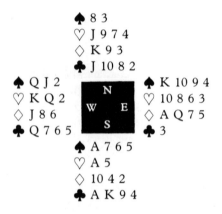

It is an interesting hand for double-dummy analysis. Clearly a trump or a spade lead puts the defenders in a better position than a red-suit lead.

Leading against Part-Scores

PROBLEM 31

Game all. Team of four.
Dealer North.

West holds   *The bidding*

♠ Q 3   W   N   E   S
♡ A 9 5 4   1D   1S   1NT
◇ 10 9 8   all pass
♣ J 9 8 2

Analysis

It is generally right to lead partner's suit unless there are strong indications to the contrary. A vulnerable overcall is normally based on a good five-card suit, but in this case South is likely to have something like A J x or K J x in spades and the lead of the spade queen could well lose a trick. It might be better if you could put partner in with a side entry and get a spade return from him. However, it is a complete guess between hearts and clubs, and if you choose the wrong suit it may cost both a trick and a tempo. A diamond lead is less likely to give up a trick but very likely to concede a vital tempo.

What about a deceptive lead of the three of spades? Since you did not support the suit declarer may read this as a singleton, and he will probably go wrong on the next round if he has A J x or K J x. Partner is likely to have several entries to help get his suit going. And if you do win the second round of spades with the queen, you will be in a good position to judge where partner's entries will be.

[81]

Marks	Spade three	10
	Spade queen	6
	Diamond ten	3
	Club two	2
	Heart four	1

Full hand

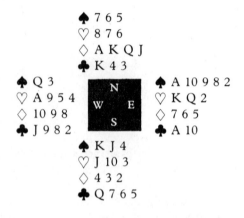

```
                      ♠ 7 6 5
                      ♡ 8 7 6
                      ◇ A K Q J
                      ♣ K 4 3
     ♠ Q 3                              ♠ A 10 9 8 2
     ♡ A 9 5 4          N               ♡ K Q 2
     ◇ 10 9 8       W       E           ◇ 7 6 5
     ♣ J 9 8 2          S               ♣ A 10
                      ♠ K J 4
                      ♡ J 10 3
                      ◇ 4 3 2
                      ♣ Q 7 6 5
```

This hand came up in a Gold Cup match and, after identical auctions, the three of spades was led in both rooms. One defender chose this card after reasoned analysis, the other because his lead convention demanded it.

PROBLEM 32

Love all.   Match-point pairs.
Dealer South.

West holds		*The bidding*			
♠	K 10	*W*	*N*	*E*	*S*
♡	A Q 5				3D
◇	Q 9 6 5	all pass			
♣	10 9 8 2				

Analysis

North is marked with quite a fair hand on this auction. At pairs, non-vulnerable, partner would have re-opened with a protective bid or double if it had been at all possible. East must be short in diamonds and it follows that he cannot have a great deal in the way of high cards.

The natural lead is the ten of clubs, which could help to develop tricks in the suit. It is a bit of a shot in the dark, however. You expect dummy to have more strength than partner, and there is a serious risk that declarer will be able to discard some losers on dummy's high clubs.

The king of spades would work well if you hit partner with good spades, but it is hardly the safest of leads.

The lead of the ace of hearts runs little risk of blowing a trick in the suit, for the king is not likely to be in the South hand. It may prove costly if dummy has the king and declarer a singleton, when a vital tempo will have been lost. Still, it is often a good idea to cash an ace against a pre-emptive auction. The big advantage is that it gives you a look at dummy and the chance to make an intelligent decision on whether to continue the suit or switch.

Marks   Heart ace   10
          Club ten   7
          Spade king   2

Full hand

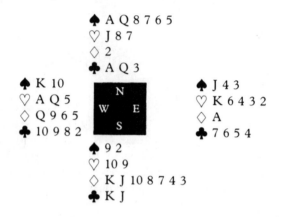

If the defenders start with three rounds of hearts, they subsequently score three trump tricks through a trump promotion.

PROBLEM 33

Game all. Match-point pairs.
Dealer North.

West holds *The bidding*

♠ A Q J 9
♡ J 6 5
♢ A 10 8
♣ 10 7 2

W	N	E	S
	1NT* —		2H
all pass			
		* 16–18	

Analysis

The lead of the ace of spades should not give much away since dummy is likely to have the king. Having started with the spade ace you can keep plugging away at the suit to develop secondary tricks or to force declarer.

A further possibility in the spade suit is to lead the queen. This will serve equally well to develop the suit and it has a psychological advantage. With K x x in dummy opposite 10 x x, declarer may play low, allowing you to steal a tempo. The lead of the queen also gives the defence more flexibility when partner has a doubleton. Against that there is the risk of losing a trick when declarer has a singleton.

A trump lead could be right if dummy has a ruffing value, but this is rather unlikely and there are too many combinations of cards in which the trump lead will cost a trick.

What about the eight of diamonds? It is sometimes good tactics to underlead an ace through the strong hand. This lead would be more attractive if your third diamond were a lower card. As it is, partner will have difficulty in reading your holding in the suit.

A club lead looks rather too passive here. If partner has a club trick it is not likely to disappear. It is in spades rather than clubs that the best chance for the defence must lie.

Marks	Ace of spades	10
	Queen of spades	10
	Eight of diamonds	3
	Two of clubs	3
	Low trump	1

Full hand

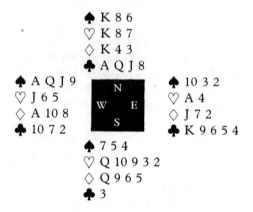

```
                ♠ K 8 6
                ♡ K 8 7
                ◇ K 4 3
                ♣ A Q J 8
  ♠ A Q J 9                    ♠ 10 3 2
  ♡ J 6 5          N           ♡ A 4
  ◇ A 10 8     W     E         ◇ J 7 2
  ♣ 10 7 2         S           ♣ K 9 6 5 4
                ♠ 7 5 4
                ♡ Q 10 9 3 2
                ◇ Q 9 6 5
                ♣ 3
```

It is hard to predict how many tricks will be made on any lead, but the spade attack certainly gives the defence a good start.

PROBLEM 34

Love all.   Match-point pairs.
Dealer East.

West holds   *The bidding*

	W	N	E	S
♠ Q 8 2	W	N	E	S
♡ K J 9 6 2			—	1NT(15–17)
◇ 8 6	—	2C	—	2H
♣ Q 9 3	—	2NT	all pass	

Analysis

North will have eight or nine points and, to judge from his use of Stayman, a four-card spade suit, while South will have his minimum of fifteen points. If South had not bid hearts there would be no reason to consider any lead other than a low heart. Now this lead is rather more risky, although it will still get the defence off to the best possible start if partner has the ace or the queen. If you know that South would not have opened one no trump with a five-card heart suit, the two of hearts may be a good shot. This will not deceive partner but may cause declarer to misjudge.

Of the other leads a spade is the most dangerous. Partner may have four spades, but dummy is *known* to have four. On balance, a spade lead must be likely to help declarer.

A passive diamond lead is worth considering. While hardly dynamic, it will at least give declarer nothing that is not his for the taking, and that is an important consideration at pairs scoring. A club lead has better attacking potential but it is also more likely to give away a trick.

Contracts of two no trumps are often touch-and-go affairs. On this hand it seems wise to select the safest possible lead and let declarer look for his own tricks.

[87]

Marks	Diamond eight	10
	Low heart	8
	Low club	4
	Low spade	1

Full hand

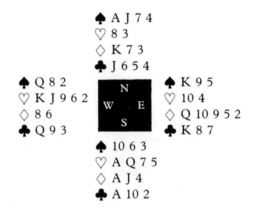

```
                    ♠ A J 7 4
                    ♡ 8 3
                    ◇ K 7 3
                    ♣ J 6 5 4
♠ Q 8 2          N              ♠ K 9 5
♡ K J 9 6 2                     ♡ 10 4
◇ 8 6          W     E          ◇ Q 10 9 5 2
♣ Q 9 3           S            ♣ K 8 7
                    ♠ 10 6 3
                    ♡ A Q 7 5
                    ◇ A J 4
                    ♣ A 10 2
```

There is no killing lead on this layout although a diamond does the least harm. Declarer can still get home if he does all the right things, but he may well go down. At any rate the diamond lead makes him work for his contract and gives no chance of an overtrick.

PROBLEM 35

Game all.   Team of four.
Dealer West.

West holds   *The bidding*

♠ K 10 5 3	W	N	E	S
♡ K 6	—	1H	—	1S
◇ 5	—	2S	—	2NT
♣ A 8 7 6 3 2	—	3S	all pass	

Analysis

The opponents appear to have stretched to the limit, and they are going to run into bad breaks in trumps and the minor suits. The only poor feature for the defence is the doubleton king of hearts under dummy's suit.

One possibility is to play for diamond ruffs, although in general this is a strategic mistake when you have a trump holding that is likely to win tricks in its own right. Partner cannot have too many entries, and even if you do get a diamond ruff the price—a weakening of the defensive diamond and trump holdings—may be too high.

The king of hearts can quickly be dismissed as too dangerous, and so can the lead of a small trump. When you have a fair trump holding it is normally right to try for a forcing defence, exerting pressure on declarer's trumps.

The lead of the ace of clubs could cost a trick in the suit, but at least it starts the defence on the right lines. With a little help in clubs from partner it may be possible to undermine dummy's trump holding. In theory the lead of a small club could gain if dummy has K x and declarer J x x, but on the bidding dummy is likely to have a singleton and it is long odds that it will be in clubs. With the overall defensive prospects looking quite good, the solid lead of the ace of clubs seems best.

Marks	Club ace	10
	Diamond five	5
	Small club	1
	Heart king	1
	Trump three	1

Full hand

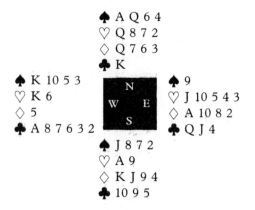

```
              ♠ A Q 6 4
              ♡ Q 8 7 2
              ◇ Q 7 6 3
              ♣ K
  ♠ K 10 5 3        N        ♠ 9
  ♡ K 6                      ♡ J 10 5 4 3
  ◇ 5        W        E      ◇ A 10 8 2
  ♣ A 8 7 6 3 2      S       ♣ Q J 4
              ♠ J 8 7 2
              ♡ A 9
              ◇ K J 9 4
              ♣ 10 9 5
```

This hand was dealt in the match between the Lancia team and Australia in 1976. Nine tricks were made when an Australian defender led the six of clubs. Either the ace of clubs or the five of diamonds defeats the contract.

6

In the Slam Zone

One might expect leading against slam contracts to be relatively easy, for in most cases the auction will have been informative and the defenders require only one or two tricks. However, the defender on lead against a slam is under heavy pressure. He knows not only that a lot of points are at stake but also that he has to get it right first time. There is no second chance when leading against a slam. An unfortunate choice of lead will usually prove to be fatal.

PROBLEM 36

N–S game.		Rubber bridge against	
Dealer East.		good opponents.	

West holds

♠ K Q 6 2
♥ J 10 9 2
♦ Q 10 2
♣ 6 5

The bidding

W	N	E	S
		—	1D
—	3C	—	4C
—	4D	—	4H
—	6D	all pass	

Analysis

There is a good chance of scoring a trump trick, and you will obviously try to set up a further trick in one of the side suits. A club lead cannot be needed for if partner has a club trick it can wait, so the choice lies between the major suits.

Many players would look no further than the king of spades, and there is a lot to be said for this. However, there are some interesting features in the auction. By agreeing diamonds North set the scene for an exchange of cue-bids, but when South bid four hearts North jumped to six diamonds, declining to mention the ace of spades which he must surely possess. His jump-shift is therefore likely to be in the lower range and, more pertinently, he probably has no heart control. With the king or a singleton heart as well as the ace of spades, he would surely have cue-bid or asked for aces with a bid of four no trumps.

Thus North's weakness appears to be in hearts rather than in spades. Of course, South could have something extra in hearts such as A Q, A K or even the singleton ace.

[93]

Conditions have to be right for a heart lead to succeed, but the spade lead is by no means automatic.

Marks   King of spades   10
           Jack of hearts   10

Full hand

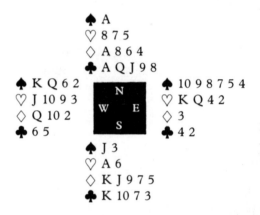

♠ A
♥ 8 7 5
♦ A 8 6 4
♣ A Q J 9 8

♠ K Q 6 2   ♠ 10 9 8 7 5 4
♥ J 10 9 3   ♥ K Q 4 2
♦ Q 10 2   ♦ 3
♣ 6 5   ♣ 4 2

♠ J 3
♥ A 6
♦ K J 9 7 5
♣ K 10 7 3

We would be quite happy to sit opposite a partner who led either a spade or a heart.

The arguments for a heart lead are valid only against good opponents, of course. Against indifferent performers there can be no point in looking for subtle bidding inferences when your eyes tell you to lead a spade.

PROBLEM 37

| Game all. | Rubber bridge against |
| Dealer South. | moderate opponents. |

| *West holds* | *The bidding* |

♠ A 8 6	*W*	*N*	*E*	*S*
♡ J 2				1S
◇ J 9 8 7 3 2	—	3D	—	3S
♣ 6 4	—	4NT	—	5C
	—	5S*	—	6S**

all pass

* *North bid 5S quickly over 5C*
** *South bid 6S slowly over 5S*

Analysis

From the auction it sounds as though the opponents may be missing two aces. South must surely have a void somewhere, since he denied an ace and yet over-ruled his partner's decision to play in five spades. If South has a useful (non-diamond) void, there are just two slim chances for the defence.

(a) You can try to give partner a diamond ruff. However, partner would surely have Lightner-doubled if void in diamonds, and if he has a singleton diamond he is unlikely to have two trumps.

(b) You can try to set up a side trick in hearts or clubs. But on the auction there is hardly room for the defenders to have a king as well as two aces and a couple of jacks.

Thus cases (a) and (b) are both remote, and you should concentrate on the situations where you have two aces to cash.

Declarer is more likely to have a club suit than a heart suit, for he might have bid the latter over three diamonds. South's heart losers could easily disappear on dummy's diamonds, and this makes a heart lead a better shot than a club.

But the sure way of locating partner's ace is to lead the ace of spades and have a look at dummy.

Marks

Ace of spades	10
Jack of hearts	5
Six of clubs	3
A diamond	2

Full hand

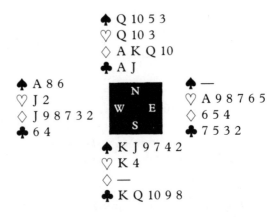

```
              ♠ Q 10 5 3
              ♡ Q 10 3
              ◇ A K Q 10
              ♣ A J
  ♠ A 8 6          N          ♠ —
  ♡ J 2        W       E      ♡ A 9 8 7 6 5
  ◇ J 9 8 7 3 2     S         ◇ 6 5 4
  ♣ 6 4                       ♣ 7 5 3 2
              ♠ K J 9 7 4 2
              ♡ K 4
              ◇ —
              ♣ K Q 10 9 8
```

Holding the wrong void, South should not have pressed on to slam, of course, but it is not infrequent for players to get into this sort of pickle.

In the Slam Zone

PROBLEM 38

Game all.
Dealer North.

Team of four.

West holds

♠ K 9 8 3
♡ K 10 8 4
◇ 10 8 6 5
♣ J

The bidding

W	N	E	S
	1C	—	1D
—	3D	—	3H
—	3S	—	4D
—	4H	—	4S
—	5D	—	6D
all pass			

Analysis

It has been a revealing auction. North has indicated reversing values with five or six clubs, four diamonds, the ace of spades and a singleton heart. South will have extra values, the heart ace, a singleton spade, and probably no high honour in clubs since he failed to bid four clubs over three spades.

South's distribution can be inferred from the fact that he has a singleton spade. If he has only four diamonds his shape must be 1–4–4–4, but a 1–4–5–3 hand is more probable and accords better with his slam ambitions.

What might partner have to give the defence two tricks? The ace of either minor suit will be enough if you lead a club. The diamond ace is hardly possible since you have worked out that partner will be void in trumps. And if he has the club ace you may defeat the contract just as easily on a different lead.

A heart lead will beat the contract if partner has as little as the queen of hearts and Q x x in clubs. Declarer will be unable to ruff all his hearts in dummy without getting in a tangle. Nor will he be able to draw all your trumps—if he does, you will be in a position to cash a heart or two when partner gains the lead in clubs.

That is the big advantage of a heart lead. A spade lead will not work in the same way, because declarer will be able to draw all your trumps and give up a club, relying on his fifth trump to control the second round of spades.

A final refinement is to lead the *king* of hearts—just in case dummy has the singleton queen.

Marks	Heart king	10
	Small heart	9
	Jack of clubs	4
	A spade	2

Full hand

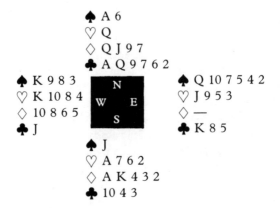

```
              ♠ A 6
              ♡ Q
              ◇ Q J 9 7
              ♣ A Q 9 7 6 2
♠ K 9 8 3          N          ♠ Q 10 7 5 4 2
♡ K 10 8 4    W       E       ♡ J 9 5 3
◇ 10 8 6 5         S          ◇ —
♣ J                           ♣ K 8 5
              ♠ J
              ♡ A 7 6 2
              ◇ A K 4 3 2
              ♣ 10 4 3
```

PROBLEM 39

N–S game.   Rubber bridge.
Dealer West.

West holds   *The bidding*

♠ Q 10 2	*W*	*N*	*E*	*S*
♡ K J	—	—	—	7NT
◇ J 8 4 3	Dbl	all pass		
♣ J 8 4 2				

Analysis

South can have no more than nine top tricks—the ace and king of spades, the heart ace, and the three top honours in both minors. The extra winners that South was counting on to bring his total up to thirteen must be in the form of long cards in a suit, probably diamonds or clubs. He might have nine cards in one of the minors, for instance, plus three aces and a king.

Whatever else he holds, South is marked with the singleton ace of hearts and a heart is the obvious lead. The question is, which card is better? The jack of hearts settles for two off; the king of hearts risks letting declarer escape for one off when dummy has the queen, but could defeat the contract by several tricks if partner has good hearts.

Leaving aside the possibility that East has seven or eight hearts (in which case he might have opened three hearts at this vulnerability), you can stipulate: (a) half of the time the king lead loses a trick—when dummy has the queen, (b) a quarter of the time the king breaks even—partner has the queen but dummy has the ten, (c) a quarter of the time the king lead results in a three-trick or greater set.

It would not be impossible to work out at the table that the lead of the jack has a slightly greater expectation of profit in the long run.

The only other lead worth considering is a spade, preferably the ten. This could hit the jackpot if dummy has something like J 8 x x and declarer the singleton ace. But this lead is far from safe. It is not inconceivable that South's bid of seven no trumps is based on ten spades plus three blank aces.

Marks Heart jack   10
         Heart king   9
         Spade ten   2

Full hand

```
              ♠ 8 6 4 3
              ♡ 10 9 4 3
              ◇ Q 9 6 5
              ♣ 10
♠ Q 10 2                      ♠ J 9 7 5
♡ K J          N              ♡ Q 8 7 6 5 2
◇ J 8 4 3    W   E            ◇ 10 7 2
♣ J 8 4 2      S              ♣ —
              ♠ A K
              ♡ A
              ◇ A K
              ♣ A K Q 9 7 6 5 3
```

The main point is that a heart is by far the best lead, there being little to choose between the king and the jack.

Early in a team game the king would perhaps be the better choice. The difference between a one-trick and a two-trick set is psychologically unimportant, but if the lead of the king produced a penalty of 1100 or more it could shatter your opponents' morale.

PROBLEM 40

Love all.   Match-point pairs.
Dealer South.

In a mixed pairs event East is a promising player lacking in experience. North is a strong player and a good psychologist, although something of a joker.

West holds	*The bidding*			
♠ 6 2	W	N	E	S
♡ Q 6 2				2S*
◇ 10 9 8 2	—	2NT**	—	3NT***
♣ K 7 6 5	—	6NT	Dbl	—
	—	7S	all pass	

*   *weak two, 7–11 points and a good six-card suit*
**   *enquiry*
*** *showing A K Q of spades*

Analysis

The auction has an Alice-in-Wonderland quality. What is going on? Can there be a logical explanation for North's actions?

North is obviously gambling but he is not the sort of player to throw points away recklessly. He must be confident that both six no trumps and seven spades will be made against the wrong opening lead. You can rely on your partner to have two cashing tricks against six no trumps—probably an ace and a king in the same suit. Hence North's gamble must be based on a solid suit of his own plus a side ace.

Now the picture is beginning to take shape. If North has a solid suit it can only be diamonds, and East must have the ace and king of hearts.

[101]

Marks   Any heart   10
                Anything else   0

Full hand

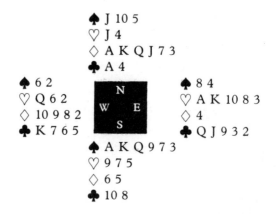

```
              ♠ J 10 5
              ♡ J 4
              ◇ A K Q J 7 3
              ♣ A 4
  ♠ 6 2                        ♠ 8 4
  ♡ Q 6 2          N          ♡ A K 10 8 3
  ◇ 10 9 8 2    W     E       ◇ 4
  ♣ K 7 6 5        S          ♣ Q J 9 3 2
              ♠ A K Q 9 7 3
              ♡ 9 7 5
              ◇ 6 5
              ♣ 10 8
```

One has to admire North's impudence. He reckoned he had a good chance of stealing a top on the board, since a club lead against six no trumps was as likely as a heart. Moreover, he judged correctly that with top hearts your partner would double six no trumps, allowing him to retreat to seven spades and transfer the problem to you.

PROBLEM 41

N–S game. Team of four.
Dealer West.

West holds *The bidding*

♠ A Q 2
♡ Q 9 8 3 2
◇ K 9 3
♣ K 10

W	N	E	S
1H	3NT*	5H	6C
all pass			

* explained as at least 6–5 in the minors
with not more than four losers

Analysis

The bidding has ascended so rapidly that it is hard to be
sure what is going on, but at this vulnerability South has
probably bid the slam to make and will have two or three likely
cover cards for North's losers. Would he count the king of
spades or the ace of hearts as cover cards? A lot would depend
on his own heart length—three or four hearts would point to
the king of spades being useful, one or two hearts would
suggest that the ace of hearts could be useful.

When North has an extreme 1–0–6–6 distribution the ace of
spades must be the best lead. It could be worth two tricks to
the defence if South does not have the spade king, for a second
spade will lock him in dummy and prevent any minor-suit
finesse. If North is 0–1–6–6, the ace of spades will cost when
South has the spade king and a minor-suit ace, but this is not
so likely.

What about the cases where North is 6–5 in the minors? (a)
1–1–6–5 or 1–1–5–6. There is no significant difference
between the ace of spades and a heart. (b) 2–0–6–5 and

2–0–5–6. The ace of spades is automatically correct when partner or dummy has the king, but is costly when declarer has the king and lacks the ace of hearts. (c) 0–2–6–5 or 0–2–5–6. The ace of spades concedes the contract when declarer has the king of spades, the ace and another heart, and a minor-suit loser. But it must be unlikely that the opponents have as many as four hearts between them.

The analysis is very complex, but the possibility of locking declarer in dummy with spade leads is hard to resist.

Marks   Ace of spades   10
          Small heart   7
          A diamond   3

Full hand

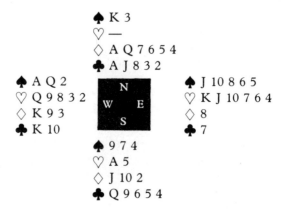

♠ K 3
♡ —
◇ A Q 7 6 5 4
♣ A J 8 3 2

♠ A Q 2
♡ Q 9 8 3 2
◇ K 9 3
♣ K 10

♠ J 10 8 6 5
♡ K J 10 7 6 4
◇ 8
♣ 7

♠ 9 7 4
♡ A 5
◇ J 10 2
♣ Q 9 6 5 4

Although a diamond lead was not discussed, it could also, in certain circumstances, lock declarer in dummy. The king of diamonds is effective here, in fact.

[104]

In the Slam Zone

PROBLEM 42

E–W game.   Team of four.
Dealer North.

West holds   *The bidding*

♠ 4
♡ Q 8 7 6 5 3
♢ 7 2
♣ A 10 5 4

W	N	E	S
	1H(1)	—	2S(2)
—	3S	—	4C(3)
—	4H(3)	—	5D(4)
—	6S	all pass	

(1) *five-card suit.*

(2) *strong single-suited hand.*

(3) *Italian-style cue-bids showing either first or second-round controls.*

(4) *first-round diamond control. With only second-round control South would have bid 4NT as a general try for slam.*

Analysis

Although North bid the final six spades it is South who has supplied most of the push towards the slam. South is marked with a good spade suit, the ace of diamonds, the king of clubs (his club control can hardly be a void since he must be short in hearts), and extra values such as secondary honours in the minor suits.

. Could partner be void in hearts? It is difficult to say. He may have refrained from making a Lightner double for fear of a retreat to six no trumps. Thus there is a case for a heart lead.

The ace of clubs would be right only in the unlikely event that partner has a singleton. What about a diamond? The idea would be to set up a trick in the suit before declarer can obtain discards. If dummy has only four cards in the minor suits, declarer may, in the absence of a diamond lead, be able to discard a diamond loser in dummy on an established club winner. But it is all rather unlikely and the diamond lead is not without risk.

It remains only to consider a trump lead. Partner can have nothing worth while in the trump suit and the lead will be completely passive. The main objection to the red-suit leads is that either could give away a vital trick.

Marks	Four of spades	10
	Seven of diamonds	6
	Small heart	5
	Ace of clubs	1

Full hand

```
                    ♠ Q 9 2
                    ♡ A K J 10 2
                    ◇ J 4
                    ♣ Q 9 2
  ♠ 4                              ♠ 8 7 5
  ♡ Q 8 7 6 5 3      N            ♡ 9 4
  ◇ 7 2          W       E        ◇ K 10 9 8 6 5
  ♣ A 10 5 4         S            ♣ 7 3
                    ♠ A K J 10 6 3
                    ♡ —
                    ◇ A Q 3
                    ♣ K J 8 6
```

On a trump lead declarer is likely to refuse the diamond finesse, although East will need to play low without batting an eye when the jack of diamonds is led.

This difficult lead problem was shown to several experts. None of them solved it but all agreed afterwards that the trump is probably the best shot.

PROBLEM 43

Game all.   Team of four.
Dealer North.

West holds   *The bidding*

♠ 4	W	N	E	S
♡ J 7 5 2		2C	—	2D
◇ K 10 6 5	—	2H	—	3NT
♣ J 10 9 4	—	4C	—	4D
	—	4NT	—	5D
	—	7NT	all pass	

Analysis

South cannot have much in the way of high cards since he gave a negative response on the first round. With a scattered eight points and a balanced hand he would have made a positive response of two no trumps. He must be just short of the values for this in view of his jump to three no trumps on the second round. He may have a queen and a jack in addition to his ace of diamonds, and North considers that this is enough for the grand slam.

North must have an enormous hand. His bidding makes sense only if it is based on a long heart suit which he expects to run. In addition, he must have the top cards in the black suits and a singleton or doubleton diamond.

How can you defend against such a holding? A spade or a club lead will give nothing away but neither will it achieve much. You have a surprise for declarer in hearts, but it will not remain a surprise for long because partner—the fool—is likely to give the show away by discarding on the first round of the suit, thereby exposing your jack to a finesse.

[107]

The only way to give yourself a real chance is to lead a diamond, aiming to take out declarer's entry before he finds out about the heart split. If North has a singleton diamond it will not matter which card you lead. But suppose North has two diamonds. In that event he must be relying on South's queen for the thirteenth trick, and obviously he could not count on the queen of diamonds for this purpose. North must know that South has a black queen, and it follows that North must have the queen of diamonds himself. In fact, to account for the placing of the contract in no trumps, North is likely to have both queen and jack of diamonds.

In that case the opening lead of a low diamond will not be good enough. To remove South's entry it will take the lead of the king.

Marks

Diamond king	10
Low diamond	7
Spade or club	1

Full hand

```
                    ♠ A K
                    ♡ A K Q 10 9 6 3
                    ◇ Q J
                    ♣ A K
    ♠ 4                          ♠ Q J 8 6 5 2
    ♡ J 7 5 2        N           ♡ —
    ◇ K 10 6 5     W   E         ◇ 9 8 4 3
    ♣ J 10 9 4       S           ♣ 8 6 3
                    ♠ 10 9 7 3
                    ♡ 8 4
                    ◇ A 7 2
                    ♣ Q 7 5 2
```

The lead of the king of diamonds does not in itself defeat the contract, but it certainly gives declarer a difficult and unusual problem. In the light of your unorthodox lead should South take a first-round heart finesse?

7

Lessons from the Champions

The problems in this final section were all faced and solved at the table by well-known international players. Many of the hands illustrate themes that have been covered in the earlier chapters, and the degree of difficulty varies.

Can you do as well as the champions?

PROBLEM 44

N–S game.   Team of four.
Dealer South.

West holds		*The bidding*		
♠ 4	*W*	*N*	*E*	*S*
♡ J 10 7 6				1S
◇ J 9 8 5 4	—	2C	—	2S
♣ A 7 5	—	3D	—	3NT
	all pass			

Analysis

A spade or a club lead is out of the question here; the choice lies between the red suits. Your longest suit is diamonds and it is often a good idea to attack dummy's second suit, which may not be too strong. All the same, the heart suit offers attractive prospects. South is not likely to have four hearts since he did not bid the suit. Nor does North sound secure in the heart department—with both red suits well stopped he might have bid no trumps himself. Although you have only four hearts, this appears to be the suit in which the opponents will be weakest.

Another way of looking at it is to reflect that South will have two or three diamonds. He did not bid hearts, he did not raise clubs and he did not bid his spades a third time, all of which builds up a picture of two or three diamonds in his hand. You are therefore unlikely to get the diamonds going, and you could easily lose a trick in the suit by leading it.

The superiority of the heart lead is clear-cut. There seems to be little to choose between the jack and the six of hearts— what is lost on the roundabouts is gained on the swings.

[111]

Marks   Heart jack or six   10
           Diamond five   2

Full hand

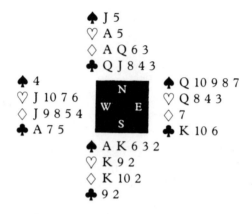

<pre>
                    ♠ J 5
                    ♡ A 5
                    ◇ A Q 6 3
                    ♣ Q J 8 4 3
    ♠ 4   ♠ Q 10 9 8 7
    ♡ J 10 7 6   N   ♡ Q 8 4 3
    ◇ J 9 8 5 4   W   E   ◇ 7
    ♣ A 7 5   S   ♣ K 10 6
                    ♠ A K 6 3 2
                    ♡ K 9 2
                    ◇ K 10 2
                    ♣ 9 2
</pre>

This hand is from the match between the U.S.A. and
Norway in the round robin of the 1970 Bermuda Bowl. The
auction was the same in both rooms, and Jim Jacoby for the
U.S.A. led the six of hearts. With the favourable club break,
declarer could have made the contract by leading twice
towards dummy's clubs, but he took his best percentage
chance by playing on spades and finished two light.

In the other room a diamond was led, allowing the ten to
score a cheap trick. With eight tricks in the bag the declarer
naturally played on clubs, ending up with eleven tricks.

PROBLEM 45

| Game all. | Pairs with Butler |
| Dealer North. | (i.m.p.) scoring. |

West holds   *The bidding*

♠ J 9 3	*W*	*N*	*E*	*S*
♡ Q 10 8 5		1C	—	1S
◇ A Q 9 4	—	4H*	—	4S
♣ K 8	all pass			

* *good raise to four spades with a control
in hearts—probably the ace.*

Analysis

Many players would lead a heart without much thought, and the lead has a lot to commend it. You would aim to establish three tricks in the red suits and hope to score an eventual trick elsewhere.

A spade lead will often give nothing away but it could be costly when partner has a high honour. Moreover, a trump lead seems altogether too passive on this hand. Your club holding is rather depressing, suggesting that after drawing trumps declarer will be able to develop dummy's club suit without difficulty.

The lead of the ace of diamonds must be inferior to a heart, since it virtually gives up all hope of defeating the contract when declarer has the diamond king.

Is there any point in leading a club? Dummy is likely to have a good five-card or longer club suit. The king of clubs could work if partner has Q x x plus a trump entry, but then a heart lead might defeat the contract anyway. What about a deceptive eight of clubs? That will put declarer under a lot of pressure, for he will fear that all the missing club honours are wrong and he will be worried about the possibility of a ruff. He is likely to put up dummy's ace of clubs, and the defenders will be well placed thereafter.

Marks	Heart five	10
	Club eight	10
	Club king	4
	Diamond ace	2
	Spade three	1

Full hand

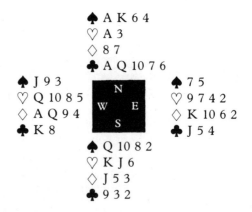

```
                    ♠ A K 6 4
                    ♡ A 3
                    ◇ 8 7
                    ♣ A Q 10 7 6
    ♠ J 9 3              N              ♠ 7 5
    ♡ Q 10 8 5       W       E          ♡ 9 7 4 2
    ◇ A Q 9 4            S              ◇ K 10 6 2
    ♣ K 8                               ♣ J 5 4
                    ♠ Q 10 8 2
                    ♡ K J 6
                    ◇ J 5 3
                    ♣ 9 3 2
```

Barnet Shenkin made the brilliant lead of the eight of clubs in the Sunday Times Invitation Pairs of 1977. This induced declarer to put up the ace of clubs and take the heart finesse in an effort to dispose of one of dummy's diamond losers.

PROBLEM 46

Game all.   Team of four.
Dealer South.

West holds		*The bidding*		

	W	*N*	*E*	*S*
♠ Q 10 2				1C
♡ Q 9 5				
◇ K J 9 6	—	1D	—	1S
♣ A Q 3	—	2H	—	2NT
	—	3NT	all pass	

Analysis

It is obvious from your array of high cards that partner can have no more than one or two points. The heart suit is the natural point of attack. South has at most three hearts, and may have the doubleton ace or king in a 4–2–2–5 hand. North will often have three hearts for his "fourth suit" bid, although he may have four. Certainly the odds favour your side having more hearts than the opponents.

How can you best attack the hearts, knowing partner to have no more than the jack in the suit? If you lead the five, East's jack will be forced out and you will subsequently be thrown in repeatedly to lead away from your honour cards.

It must be better to start with the queen of hearts, a lead that has several advantages. In the first place, declarer may misjudge the lie of the cards and neglect to hold up. More importantly, if South does get it wrong you will have created an unexpected entry for partner, which he will use to good effect by leading through South's honour cards.

Are there any other leads worth considering? The diamond king might pin a singleton queen or ten when declarer's shape is 4–3–1–5. But there is a risk of finding South with A x opposite Q 10 x x x.

In the spade suit the queen is again the best choice, but this is a highly dangerous lead when declarer is known to have a genuine spade suit.

Marks		
	Queen of hearts	10
	King of diamonds	6
	Five of hearts	2
	Six of diamonds	2
	Queen of spades	1

Full hand

```
                  ♠ K 7 4
                  ♡ A 10 4
                  ◇ A 8 7 4 3
                  ♣ 7 2
  ♠ Q 10 2         N          ♠ 8 6 5
  ♡ Q 9 5       W     E       ♡ J 7 3 2
  ◇ K J 9 6                   ◇ 10 5
  ♣ A Q 3          S          ♣ 8 6 5 4
                  ♠ A J 9 3
                  ♡ K 8 6
                  ◇ Q 2
                  ♣ K J 10 9
```

This hand was used in 1975 by Jeremy Flint to illustrate his "Bols Bridge Tip", which read: "Instead of stolidly pushing out an unimaginative small card from three or four to an honour, you should consider whether to lead the honour."

If a small heart is led the contract will romp home, but on the lead of the queen of hearts declarer will surely misguess and go down. The king of diamonds gives the defenders a sporting chance but declarer is likely to come out on top.

PROBLEM 47

Game all. Team of four.
Dealer North.

West holds *The bidding*

♠ 9 5 3	W	N	E	S
♡ A 10 7 6		—	2D*	Dbl**
◇ A 10 3	2S***	3D	3H	3S
♣ 10 7 6	—	4S	all pass	

* *Multi-coloured two diamonds, subsequently shown to be 6–10 points with a fair, six-card heart suit.*
** *16 or more points with at least one major suit.*
*** *Shows willingness to play in three hearts if East has a weak two-bid in hearts.*

Analysis

At this vulnerability East will have a fairly respectable heart suit, yet he lacked the strength to open one heart. Clearly it is no good expecting him to supply two defensive tricks in the side suits.

What about the diamond position? To bid the suit at the three-level North will have at least five diamonds and probably six. There must be a fair chance that East will have a singleton diamond.

The trouble with a passive lead such as a spade or a club is that even if partner has some honour cards in the black suits they will be well-placed for declarer. And a forcing defence can hardly work. Trumps are breaking evenly, and declarer will be able to take second- or third-round heart ruffs in dummy if necessary.

It would be quite fortunate to find partner with a singleton diamond, but this seems by far the best chance for the defence.

Marks

Diamond ace	10
Heart ace	4
A club	1
A trump	1

Full hand

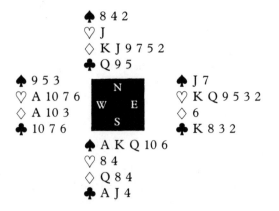

```
                    ♠ 8 4 2
                    ♡ J
                    ◇ K J 9 7 5 2
                    ♣ Q 9 5
     ♠ 9 5 3          N          ♠ J 7
     ♡ A 10 7 6                  ♡ K Q 9 5 3 2
     ◇ A 10 3       W    E       ◇ 6
     ♣ 10 7 6         S          ♣ K 8 3 2
                    ♠ A K Q 10 6
                    ♡ 8 4
                    ◇ Q 8 4
                    ♣ A J 4
```

This hand came up in the 1975 Camrose match between England and Scotland. One of the authors was on the receiving end when Tony Priday made the fine lead of the ace of diamonds to put the contract two down. On a non-diamond lead the game is unbeatable.

PROBLEM 48

Game all.   Team of four.
Dealer West.

West holds   *The bidding*

	♠ K 6 5 3	*W*	*N*	*E*	*S*
	♡ 8 4	—	1S(1)	—	1NT(2)
	◇ A 10 8 5	—	2D(3)	—	2NT(4)
	♣ 7 6 2	—	3NT	all pass	

(1) *Five-card suit, 11–15 points.*
(2) *Forcing.*
(3) *May be only a three-card suit.*
(4) *About 11 points, balanced, non-forcing.*

Analysis

The opponents have a maximum of 26 points, and on this auction South will not have a singleton. There is consequently no chance of five diamond tricks and no need to lead the suit— a diamond away from the ace through a holding of three or four cards in dummy would be highly dangerous.

All the indications point to the selection of as passive a lead as possible. A club is superior to a heart since the defenders are likely to have greater length in clubs. If dummy is 5–3–3–2 (a likely shape) the doubleton must be in clubs—otherwise North's rebid after his partner's forcing response of one no trump would have been two clubs, not two diamonds. Apart from that, a trebleton lead is usually preferable to a doubleton and is less easily misread by partner.

The lead of a small spade might be passive enough, but it could be costly if declarer happened to have the ace over partner's doubleton jack.

Marks

A club	10
Eight of hearts	7
Small spade	3
Five of diamonds	1

Full hand

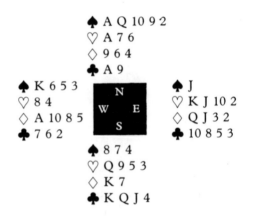

```
            ♠ A Q 10 9 2
            ♡ A 7 6
            ◇ 9 6 4
            ♣ A 9
♠ K 6 5 3        N        ♠ J
♡ 8 4       W        E    ♡ K J 10 2
◇ A 10 8 5       S        ◇ Q J 3 2
♣ 7 6 2                   ♣ 10 8 5 3
            ♠ 8 7 4
            ♡ Q 9 5 3
            ◇ K 7
            ♣ K Q J 4
```

This hand is from the round robin match between the
U.S.A. and China in the 1970 Bermuda Bowl. Bob Hamman
for the U.S.A. made the good lead of the seven of clubs.

Declarer could still have made his contract (by cashing four
clubs and then leading a spade to the queen, for instance), but
in practice he went down. As it happens, East's strength is in
hearts and an initial heart lead gives declarer no chance.

PROBLEM 49

Game all.   Team of four.
Dealer South.

West holds   *The bidding*

♠ 10 6 5 2   W   N   E   S
♡ J 9   1C(1)
◇ 8 3   —   1NT(2) —   2H(3)
♣ 7 6 5 3 2   —   2S(4) —   2NT(5)
                    —   4H(6) —   6H
                    all pass

(1) *Precision, 16 or more points.*
(2) *8–13 points, balanced.*
(3) *Asking bid, showing five or more hearts.*
(4) *Denies trump support as good as Q x x and denies four
    controls (Ace = 2, king = 1).*
(5) *Waiting.*
(6) *Shows four small hearts.*

Analysis

South must be relying more on high cards than on
distribution for his twelve tricks. With a second five-card suit,
for instance, he would have bid the suit rather than use the
waiting bid of two no trumps. That is just about the only
inference to be drawn—there is no clue as to where the
opponents' weakness may lie.

Of the plain suit leads a club is perhaps the most passive, for
the simple reason that your length in the suit reduces the risk
of doing damage. Of course, a club lead could resolve a guess
about the position of the queen and could pave the way for the

discard of a loser in another suit. In the absence of better information, all plain suit leads are dangerous.

In contrast, a trump lead is completely safe. You know that partner has no more than two hearts and, no matter what these are, you cannot give away a trick in the suit. In fact, if you lead the nine of hearts and find partner with a doubleton queen or king, you may give declarer a nasty guess on the second round, creating a losing option where none existed before.

Marks

Trump nine	10
Trump jack	6
A club	4
A spade	3
A diamond	3

Full hand

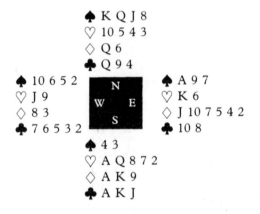

Benito Garozzo led the nine of hearts against this slam (reached by a different route) in the 1976 World Team Olympiad at Monte Carlo, and the declarer lost a trump trick as well as the ace of spades.

PROBLEM 50

Love all.   Rubber bridge against
Dealer South.   good opponents.

West holds   *The bidding*

♠ A J 5 2   W   N   E   S
♡ K 10 8 5 2   1S
◇ Q 6 3   —   2C   —   3S
♣ 6   —   4D   —   4H
                  —   4S   all pass

Analysis

What is partner likely to have on this auction? Obviously
very little. For his three-spade rebid, opener will have six or
seven spades headed by K Q 10, the ace of hearts, a high club
honour and another honour card—either a second club
honour or the king of diamonds. Responder must have several
key cards to justify his slam try—two or three small trumps,
the diamond ace, and either an excellent club suit or fair clubs
with the diamond king.

There is no chance of establishing a forcing defence when
declarer has so many trumps, so you must plan to score your
two natural trump tricks, a trick in one of the red suits, and a
club ruff. Will partner have a card of entry to give you that
club ruff?

The most likely card for partner to hold is the queen of
hearts, but the lead of a low heart can hardly work unless East
has the jack as well, for you know the ace of hearts to be with
South. Dummy has the ace of diamonds, so a diamond lead
will work in the unlikely event that partner has the king.

The lead of the singleton club is better than either of these
because it gives you both chances. You can win the first trump
and decide, in the light of what you can see in dummy,
whether to switch to a heart or a diamond.

[123]

Your main hopes must rest on finding partner with the queen of hearts, however, and the best shot is to lead the king of hearts. Declarer will not dare to hold up for fear of a club switch. He will take his ace and play trumps. You can win and switch to your club, and eventually put partner in with that hypothetical queen of hearts to give you a ruff.

Marks

Heart king	10
Club six	7
Small heart	5
A diamond	3

Full hand

```
              ♠ 8 7
              ♡ J 9 3
              ◇ A K
              ♣ A J 10 8 5 4
♠ A J 5 2          N          ♠ 4
♡ K 10 8 5 2              ♡ Q 7 4
◇ Q 6 3     W       E     ◇ 10 9 8 5 4 2
♣ 6               S        ♣ 9 7 3
              ♠ K Q 10 9 6 3
              ♡ A 6
              ◇ J 7
              ♣ K Q 2
```

The brilliant lead of the king of hearts was found at the table by Michael Rosenberg. The play developed exactly as he had foreseen and the contract went one down.

Note that it is not good enough for West to start with the singleton club and switch to the king of hearts when in with the ace of spades. Alerted by this sequence of plays, declarer will spot the danger and hold up his ace of hearts.